IS THIS KID "CRAZY"?

Understanding Unusual Behavior

Westminster Press Books by
Margaret O. Hyde

Is This Kid "Crazy"? Understanding
Unusual Behavior

Cry Softly! The Story of Child Abuse

IS THIS KID "CRAZY"?

Understanding Unusual Behavior

Margaret O. Hyde

THE WESTMINSTER PRESS
Philadelphia

BOOK DESIGN BY ALICE DERR

Published by The Westminster Press ®
Philadelphia, Pennsylvania

PRINTED IN THE UNITED STATES OF AMERICA
9 8 7 6 5 4 3 2

For Lisette Dyer-Baxter RN,
who cares

Library of Congress Cataloging in Publication Data

Hyde, Margaret Oldroyd, 1917–
  Is this kid "crazy"?

11-85

  Bibliography: p.
  Includes index.
  SUMMARY: Discusses possible causes, symptoms, and remedies of several types of mental illness that affect children and adolescents including autism, depression, schizophrenia, and anorexia nervosa. Also considers a variety of emotional problems that cause withdrawal, fear of school, enuresis, and social manipulation.
  1. Child psychopathology—Juvenile literature.
  2. Adolescent psychopathology—Juvenile literature.
  3. Emotional problems of children—Juvenile literature.
  4. Emotional problems of adolescents—Juvenile literature.
  [1. Mental illness. 2. Emotional problems] I. Title.
  RJ499.H93 1983   618.92'89   83-16916
  ISBN 0-664-32707-9

C. 2

Contents

Foreword
by Elizabeth Held Forsyth, M.D.   7

1. Would You Know a Crazy Person
   If You Met One?   9
2. Betty Jane, Timmy, and Maria   16
3. What's Wrong with This Child?   26
4. The World of Autistic Children   34
5. Schizophrenia   42
6. Depression   53
7. Anorexia Nervosa and Other Eating
   Disorders   60
8. Weird, but Dangerous?   67

   Mental Health Terms   77
   Suggestions for Further Reading   83
   For Further Information   85
   *Adolescent Clinics in the United
      States and Canada*   87

Foreword

Do you know someone who behaves so differently that a description of weird, troubled, or crazy seems to fit? Such people may make you feel uncomfortable or frightened, so you may be tempted to avoid them. Perhaps you know someone who is the victim of cruel remarks or jokes because that person does not seem to fit with the rest of the group. Cruelty of this sort is commonly based on fear, lack of knowledge, or insensitivity about the strange person's problems, but such actions can hurt badly.

Many children are struggling to overcome emotional problems, but their progress is made more difficult by people who reject them and force them into isolation. Many young people lack understanding of what it means to be mentally ill or how to help those who are emotionally disturbed. Even the families of children with serious problems often fail to recognize their symptoms at an early stage, believing that the difficulties are "just a phase" and will be outgrown.

Perhaps you have a friend who has a schizophrenic parent. Perhaps your mother is suffering from a serious bout of depression, or a neighbor's child is afraid to go to school. Perhaps you suspect that one of your friends is alternately starving herself by dieting, and then indulging in eating binges. How can you help?

Whether you come in contact only briefly with someone who suffers from mental illness, or whether you live in a family where emotional disturbance causes frequent disruption, you will find helpful information in this book. It is an interesting and practical guide for those who want facts about some of the problems of mental illness and other unusual behaviors.

ELIZABETH HELD FORSYTH, M.D.
Child Psychiatrist

1
Would You Know a Crazy Person If You Met One?

Do you know a crazy person? People who seem "different" in their behavior are often called weird, bonko, crazy, nutty, and other names, but almost everyone is sometimes a little crazy and occasionally does strange things. Have you ever wondered if you might be crazy? Perhaps you have a friend or a parent who seems weird. Just what does "crazy" mean? Are crazy people dangerous? Can they be helped? These are just some of the questions many people have about themselves and their friends.

"She's crazy as a loon." "You're driving me crazy." "I'm crazy about Sally." "What a crazy idea!" These expressions are meaningful to almost everyone. However, defining a crazy person is difficult.

Actually, there is no accurate definition of the word "crazy." If you lived on an island in the Bering Sea, where Eskimos speak a language known as Yupik, you would say that a person who hears voices or screams at things that do not exist is *nuthkavihak*. If you were a member of the Yorubas who live in rural Nigeria, you would use a different word to describe a person who laughs when there is nothing to laugh at, but you would mean much the same thing. People around the world who exhibit strange patterns of behavior are referred to as crazy in the language of their native land.

Doctors and others who work in the field of mental health really do not like the word "crazy," but many of them find themselves using it in a slangy way just the same. Even when there are more accurate and specific definitions for abnormal mental conditions, the word "crazy" still finds its way into descriptions of people who behave or think very differently from most. There is no completely satisfactory definition of mental illness, nor are there any sharp boundaries for specific mental disorders. For example, someone may be suffering from a combination of depression and anorexia nervosa. Nor is there any sharp boundary between being mentally ill and not mentally ill. A person who is mentally ill, however, is usually someone who is very disturbed. There is no doubt that a person who is psychotic, one who is not in touch with reality and draws incorrect conclusions from what he or she sees and hears, is a mentally ill person.

Sometimes there is no clear line between people who act crazy and those who behave in so-called normal ways. A troubled person may have learned to hide hurts in a different way from most people and it may be a way that society finds very strange, but it is a way of acting that protects the troubled person. All people fight for survival in their own special ways. In some cases, the emotional walls they build are so thick that others cannot reach them.

Consider Sally, a child who can speak but seldom does. When she looks at other people, she seems to be looking through them. She never responds to the love that they express. Sally bangs her head against the floor hour after hour, and when she tires of this, she kicks the wall. If her shoe comes off, she kicks the wall with her bare feet even after both her feet and the wall are smeared with blood. No one understands her rage or her terror, for she cannot express them in the usual ways. Most people say that Sally is a very different child, and they feel uncomfortable when they are with her. Some children and adults are afraid of her wild behavior. Even the doctors and the people who care for Sally do not fully understand why she behaves the way she does, but they believe that she suffers from a disorder known as autism. The caretaker who is working to reach her behind the wall Sally has built resents the fact that some people call her crazy.

No matter what labels are used, everyone agrees that there is a great need for more understanding of the miserable, unhappy, defiant, or withdrawn children who are mentally disturbed.

The understanding of troubled minds has come a long way since the time when strange or crazy behavior was blamed on demons and spirits. Through many years and in many places, harsh means were used in attempts to drive away the devils. Steaming, branding, purging, and cutting were popular ways of trying to get rid of the devils that were believed to be the cause of insanity. Even today, there are some people who believe that certain children are possessed by demons that can

11

be driven out by special religious ceremonies known as exorcism.

Through the years, people with deranged feelings, strange behavior, and unusual ways of thinking have been the subject of much torture, sometimes in the name of treatment. London's Bethlehem Hospital, originally founded in 1247, was converted to an asylum in the sixteenth century. Here, women were chained by the ankles to a long wall. Many men were attached by the neck to a vertical bar. One man was known to have been kept that way for a dozen years even as late as the eighteenth century. The corrupted name of Bethlehem Hospital, Bedlam, became a byword for cruelty to the mentally ill.

It was not uncommon for people to visit asylums and watch the antics of the insane. Visitors were charged a small fee for the privilege of learning about the mad people and for being entertained by their strange behavior.

Madness or insanity, as it was commonly called, was not regarded as a medical problem until the early nineteenth century. About that time, a movement began to release people from captivity, remove their chains, and give them more humane treatment. Scientific efforts were made to understand possible causes for such behavior, but many mysteries remain even today. Compassionate treatment moved forward, but many of the old attitudes remain. While some cases of mental illness provoke sympathy, it is difficult to feel anything but horror for the very small percentage of people who commit violent acts that cause great tragedy.

Disturbed minds both repel and fascinate. Stories in newspapers about mentally ill children who have been kept in hiding by their families appeal to many readers. Some disturbed people have become leaders through a strange combination of exotic ways and personal charisma. Adolf Hitler is an example of one whose emotional illness played a part in his power. Charles Manson was famous as a leader of a group known as a family. He held his followers together and ruled them with authority that culminated in their participation in shocking and bizarre murders. The stabbing and bludgeoning actions of the family were actions that many people considered to be as insane as they felt Manson was. Jim Jones held the power of life and death over the hundreds of followers who committed suicide at his command in Jonestown in 1978. Throughout history, a number of deranged individuals have controlled large groups of people in the name of religion and led them in both good and bad activities.

Many troubled children in today's world are treated with more understanding and compassion than such children received in the past, but there are no easy answers to their problems or the problems of those who care about them. This is especially true when children who are frightened or angered lash out physically at others. Even when one tries to understand that such a physically ferocious child may be acting out his or her own terror, those who love such a child are often filled with despair.

Many times the brothers and sisters, the mothers and the fathers of mentally ill people experience shame, guilt, anger, sadness, or resentment about the disturbed member of the family. The fact that many individuals reject and fear the mentally ill without trying to understand them adds to the family burden.

Experts have never found the answer to the question When does normal behavior become abnormal? Some estimates indicate that more than half the people in the world suffer from some emotional disturbance. Then this kind of suffering technically becomes the normal. But when people plunge deeply into the nightmare of mental illness, they bring about major changes in the lives of their families and all who try to help them. Weird behavior is likely to affect everyone at some time or other, either directly or indirectly.

According to Dr. Leon Shapiro, coauthor of *You Are Not Alone,* many people living today will most certainly have occasion to use the services of a mental health professional for themselves or a family member.

About one out of ten persons is at least somewhat disabled by mental illness. Between 1 percent and 10 percent of the people in any country of the world suffer from the disease of schizophrenia at any one time. About 20 percent of the people in the world suffer from a kind of depression that is much more severe than feeling blue for a day or two. For some, depression is so severe that they spend many of their days just lying in bed. No one knows how many individuals at some point in their lives suffer from various mild forms of mental disturbance caused by emotional conflicts. It probably includes a very large percentage of the population.

Children are no longer considered miniature adults who are expected to think and react as adults do. During the years between birth and middle adolescence they develop ways of thinking, reasoning, and feeling. Disturbed children manifest their problems in different ways from disturbed adults. Many children have more than the normal share of emotional difficulties during their growing years. As many as 15 percent of the children in the United States may be abnormal. No matter how one labels the disorders of childhood and adolescence, they do exist.

Knowing more about conditions that trouble the mind can help everyone. You may find stories in this book that make you think of people you know. You may even recognize some things that you feel or do. Few, if any, people go through life without feeling or acting crazy at some time or other. Many so-called crazy people have made major contributions to society. Certainly, reading this book should help you to understand your own feelings better and to learn a little more about the troubled people who touch your life.

2
Betty Jane, Timmy, and Maria

Sara was thinking about a career in some kind of hospital work, but she told her adviser that she did not want to become involved with any crazy people. She explained that she had once met a person who had just been discharged from a mental hospital and she found herself very uncomfortable. Sara's cousin had suffered from schizophrenia. Sara stayed away from the house where he lived after she heard that he imagined that people were plotting against him. He was trying to persuade anyone who visited to join his army. He thought he was the general.

Sara could not explain why she only wanted to help people who were physically ill. Perhaps it was because she felt they could not help being sick, while people who suffered from mental illness somehow seemed responsible for their own problems. Sara was one of the people who said, "Pull yourself together. If you don't straighten out, you will have no one to blame but yourself." "You have to help yourself" was another of her favorite expressions.

Sara is like many people who feel that mentally ill people must be that way because of their own willfulness. They do not take into account the fact that some mental illness is caused by genetic factors, by organic disease, by chemicals from the environment, by family difficulties, or by combinations of many things over which people have no control. Being emotionally ill is usually a very unpleasant experience. One man describes it in the following way: "I felt all this tumult of madness—all this stark, lonely living which is worse than death—and the pain, the futility, and hopelessness of it all—and the endlessness, the eternity."

It helps people to feel less responsible for those who are disturbed if they can believe that such illness comes to those who do not exercise control. If Sara can believe that people are responsible for their own mental illness, she has less fear that something like this will happen to her. If mental illness is beyond a person's control, it is a threat.

Sara changed her attitude about working with emotionally ill people after she read the following cases that her adviser who had been a social worker shared with her.

Betty Jane was absent from school again. The other fifth-graders wondered why she was sick so often. She was not the type of person who skipped school. In fact, she seemed overly conscientious about her schoolwork and concerned about doing well. Peggy knew the reason for her friend's absence. It had nothing to do with physical illness, although Betty Jane often had headaches or stomach aches that prevented her from going to school or on overnight trips with the Girl Scout troop.

17

Several times friends at school asked Peggy if Betty Jane was weird. Peggy sometimes wondered why Betty Jane would let a minor ailment like a headache stop her from joining in the fun of a field trip. She learned that Betty Jane had become very anxious about going to school, so nervous, in fact, that she simply could not go at all. It wasn't really the headaches, and it wasn't that she hated school, or even that she felt so nervous when she got there. She did not know what made her so uncomfortable, and her friend was puzzled by her refusal to attend school. After all, she acted normal in every other respect; she wasn't weird, but this behavior certainly was weird.

Betty Jane's mother became worried about her. Even though Peggy was bringing homework assignments to her friend, she was missing so much work by staying home that she might have to repeat the grade next year. Betty Jane's mother was a pleasant person and a caring mother, but Peggy thought she seemed to be overprotective. She always worried about whether Betty Jane was dressed warmly enough, or whether she was eating properly, or if she had remembered her bus fare. At the beginning of the year, when Betty Jane had been going to school, her mother became anxious when she was delayed or when she stopped at a friend's house. Peggy supposed that it was probably natural for Betty Jane's mother to be overly concerned about her, because her brother had been hit by a car on his way home one afternoon and had spent a long time in the hospital. But that had happened three years ago, and besides, Betty Jane was not so reckless as John was.

Betty Jane's parents did not know how to get her back to school. No amount of cajoling could make her go. So they finally decided that perhaps they needed some counseling. Betty Jane was reluctant to talk to anyone about this problem, because it was embarrassing to discuss personal matters with strangers and because she felt that no one else could give her an answer. She would really have preferred to work things out herself. It turned out that the counseling sessions did give the family some answers. Betty Jane was able to talk about some fears that she had not discussed before. She worried about her father, who had recently received a promotion. His new job kept him away from home much of the time. He often traveled by plane. Betty Jane also worried that her mother might have an accident or that a burglar would break into the house. Somehow she felt safer staying close to her mother rather than leaving the house.

Although it was clear to Betty Jane's friends, it was not so clear to her mother that she was overly anxious about Betty Jane. She realized that she had been transferring her own fears to her daughter. This mother had been neglected when she was a child and had moved from one foster home to another. As though to try to make up for her bad experiences, she showered extra attention and concern on her own children. She also found it hard to say no to them and to enforce any rules, because she was afraid that she might lose their love. Lack of security and lack of love from her parents made her worry too much about depriving her own children. In addition, it was very difficult for her to encourage Betty Jane to overcome her fears of becoming independent and doing things without her parents, because a part of her did not want Betty Jane to grow up and leave her.

When both Betty Jane and her parents were able to talk about some of their worries, somehow they were better able to face their fears. Her mother stopped trying to protect her so much and encouraged her to do things on her own. Betty Jane went back to school and became more adventurous. Even when her classmates asked her why she had been away so long, she wasn't too embarrassed to explain.

The children in Timmy's class teased him about his problems.

"Timmy's crazy." You could hear his classmates say this almost any day of the week about this small, weird boy who seemed willing to do anything that anyone asked him to do. One day, when Timmy was walking home from school, two of his classmates challenged him to walk across a plank over a stream. They knew the plank was rotted and that he would probably fall into the stream. No one in the group would think of walking across, since it seemed obvious that the plank would break, but they bet that Timmy would do it. And, of course, when he tried it, he fell into the water, scratched his leg, and tore his new pants.

No one really thought much about why Timmy did anything that people asked him to do. One day, a boy told him that he would be invited to join the gang if he learned how to smoke. The boy knew that Timmy would get sick if he smoked the three cigarettes he insisted upon, but Timmy thought learning to smoke would make him popular, so he struggled through them. The next day, Timmy stayed home from school, and when he did return, the gang did not really accept him anyhow. They just laughed and said they would let him know what the next part of the initiation would be.

Some of the people in the class felt sorry for Timmy. The girl who lived next door to Timmy said that he had a crazy mother. His mother was seldom home, and his father had left the family when Timmy was very young. Sometimes, Timmy had to stay home to take care of his mother. When he came back to school after a long absence, his teacher complained because he never brought the proper excuse. The teacher thought about sending a social worker to Timmy's home to find out why his clothing was so dirty, but she was afraid someone might think that she was interfering with the privacy of a family. Besides, there was no physical sign of child abuse.

Talking to Timmy did no good. He claimed that everything was fine at home. But when he fell off the rotten plank, there was no one home to care about his scratches or his torn clothing. Timmy mended them as best he could. Rather than blame others for his fall, Timmy blamed himself for being clumsy. He decided he would try harder to please. Maybe the kids would stop calling him crazy Timmy if he could really manage to do the things they asked him to do.

Even though a few boys and girls felt sorry for Timmy, no one in the class really understood why Timmy seemed weird. No one in the class knew that he had to do most of the housecleaning, get the meals, shop for groceries and for his mother, and try to do his homework after he calmed his crying parent. No one really understood that the reason Timmy tried so hard to please the people in his class was that he needed someone to be his friend.

One day, some boys who were hanging around the school grounds tried to get several of the eighth-graders to carry drugs to a certain store for them. They made it clear that anyone under the age of sixteen would not get into very much trouble if he or she were caught. But most of the people who were asked remembered a boy who had left school after he was caught carrying drugs. No one was sure what had happened to him after he was held at the detention center waiting for his hearing in juvenile hall. Then someone got the idea that maybe Timmy would do what they were afraid to do. They could make that the next part of his initiation into the gang.

Several of the boys called Timmy over to the edge of the school grounds. They told him about the next part of the initiation and asked him if he would meet them after school for beer sessions. Timmy had never drunk beer, but he was willing to try anything if only people would be friends with him. At the beer session, Timmy was introduced to the older boys. He was told where to take the secret package, not to open the package, but to give it to the man in the store.

Timmy delivered the secret package and enjoyed the fuss the gang made of him when he returned. He was going to be the official messenger of the gang. Timmy had an idea that he was doing something wrong, but now he had some friends. The boys who were afraid to deliver the drugs made a fuss over him, since they were getting some free beer for making the arrangement. For a while, everyone seemed happy. Since most of the people in the class did not know what Timmy was doing, they wondered why he suddenly seemed to be having such a good time and was accepted by the gang. Then, one day, Timmy told the girl who sat next to him in math class what he was doing. Timmy thought this girl would help him if he got in trouble.

The word soon spread around the class, and "weird Timmy" seemed crazier than ever to almost everyone who heard that he was willing to carry drugs just to be a member of the gang. When one of the girls who felt sorry for Timmy told her mother what was happening, the mother contacted a friend who was a social worker. He reached Timmy before his actions were discovered by the police.

After Timmy made friends with the social worker, he felt better. He did not really want to break the law, but he wanted someone to pay attention to him. The social worker explained that there were better ways of getting help. He talked with Timmy several hours a week and found some help for his mother, too.

After a while, Timmy lost his reputation for doing anything that anyone asked him to do. He learned that the other children liked him for just being himself and not trying so hard to act the way he thought others wanted him to act. After a while, people began to realize that he was not weird. Some of them even wondered if they had been a little weird because they ignored his problems earlier in the year.

Sara's adviser had been a social worker in a clinic

before she came to the school, so she was able to share a case study about someone with serious problems. She changed the name of the girl before letting Sara read about her, but she assured Sara that the things that happened were very real.

Maria's roommate brought her to the local mental health clinic, where Maria asked to be "put away." Her roommate was disgusted with her and blamed her for not helping with the work or contributing to the cost of the apartment. She had no money because she was "too lazy" to hold her job as a cleaning woman. During the last few months, this eighteen-year-old girl had refused to eat more than snacks, seldom got out of bed, and had long periods of weeping.

After interviews by the therapist at the clinic, Maria's background began to emerge. It was discovered that Maria's life had been a stormy one. She was born and brought up in rural Puerto Rico as part of a large family. Maria was the father's favorite child, the one who went with him on fishing trips and to ball games, and helped him on the farm. When Maria was twelve years old, her father was shot in a fight with a neighbor and died in Maria's arms. This violent death left a trauma that she never fully overcame.

When Maria's background is considered, it is less difficult to understand her "laziness" and her spells of weeping. Yet, many people would have more aversion to Maria than to someone who was suffering from heart disease.

Sara's attitude about emotional illness changed somewhat after she considered the cases of Betty Jane, Timmy, and Maria, but she still felt that she would not like to include the care of such people in her work at the hospital. Sara still held some of the same beliefs that are common myths.

Myth one: Most mentally ill people are dangerous.

Myth two: Once crazy, always crazy.

Myth three: Mental illness is a sign of personal weakness.

Myth four: All mentally ill people are irrational and have lost control over their behavior.

How many of these myths have you believed?

3
What's Wrong
with This Child?

Billy is a two-year-old who races through the house, upsetting wastebaskets, throwing toys at furniture, and hitting out at anything or anyone in his way. He has poured his milk in the dishwasher, broken the television screen, and put his shoes in the garbage. Since Billy is only two years old, some people say he is just a very active child. Other people say that Billy needs help with his feelings. Perhaps all this destruction is a way of asking for more attention and expressions of love. Or, if he gets plenty of attention and love, Billy may have some kind of emotional problem.

Conditions of the mind and emotions cannot be measured the way most physical illnesses can be tested. A thermometer can show a fever that warns of various kinds of sickness; other tests can show the presence of various kinds of viruses or bacteria. X-rays can show the presence of a growth or the break in a bone. In some cases of brain damage, there are tests that indicate something is wrong, but the causes of many kinds of mental illness are not so easily identified. Psychiatrists and psychologists depend on the results of many verbal and written tests, along with the behavior of the person in question as well as observations of families, teachers, and employers. Their personal biases may influence their way of describing behavior to a greater degree than when there are objective and specific tests to determine a person's ailment. No wonder there is much disagreement about labels for some kinds of mental illness. Is this child autistic or suffering from childhood schizophrenia? Some doctors say there is no such thing as childhood depression, while others disagree emphatically. The disorders of children may be given the same names as those applied to adults, but the behavior problems may be quite different.

Many parents grow upset by problems that are really quite common among children and by troubles that will go away by themselves. For example, fighting, cruelty, defiance of authority, excessive guilt feelings, withdrawal, and temper tantrums are problems that may be signs of real disturbance, or they may just be phases through which a child is passing. Most children improve without help from mental health professionals, but there are cases when they do not. When a child shows symptoms not common for his or her age level, some kind of emotional disturbance may be present.

One childhood disorder that is common and *may* be related to emotional disturbances is bed-wetting. Tommy's mother became alarmed when he wet the bed several nights after he started first grade. She felt that he should be able to control himself, and she reacted by calling him a baby. Tommy's mother did not realize that about one in seven of the children enrolling in school for the first time have similar problems. The guilt feelings, distress, and frustrations that arose from Tommy's problems were more serious than his bed-wetting.

Enuresis is the technical name for the involuntary discharge of urine after the age at which most children are toilet trained. Each year, about 12 to 15 percent of children who have this problem outgrow it without any treatment. About 10 percent of children are bed wetters at the age of ten, but only 3 percent of fifteen-year-olds have this problem.

While many people consider enuresis a psychological disorder, there may well be other reasons for the problem. Immature muscular control, an obstruction, infection, allergy, and unusually deep sleep are some of the reasons for wetting the bed.

Bobby began wetting his bed after his new sister arrived. This is common among young children at such times, but Bobby's case included other problems. He would not believe that his mother had gone to the hospital to have a baby, nor would he look at the baby after she came home. He crawled into the crib that was set up for the infant, and he urinated when he was scolded. Bobby's parents took him to see a psychiatrist, who suggested that Bobby considered the presence of the new baby as unfair. His enuresis was part of deep underlying emotional conflicts that were resolved only after a long period of treatment.

Some experts believe that any attempt to cure persistent enuresis without getting to the cause of emotional problems is wrong. Others believe that the popular treatment of using a pad and a buzzer method to teach self-control is all that is needed. When a child sleeps on such a pad, the first few drops of urine cause a buzzer to ring. This wakens the child, enabling him or her to get up and go to the bathroom. When bed-wetting is due to the fact that cues for waking in response to bladder tension have not been well learned, this system teachs self-control. The bell and pad method is reported to have worked well in most cases, with no emotional problems being substituted.

Encopresis, or soiling by elimination of solid matter at the wrong time or place, is considered more likely to be the result of an emotional disturbance than enuresis. Some children withhold bowel movements or alternate between inappropriate elimination and withholding. Since the period of toilet training is an opportunity for a child to resist the demands of parents, some children use this way to show their hostility. Many such children are found to be neat and orderly and to guard against any display of fighting back other than their expression of hostility through soiling. In some cases, there are physical causes for this problem.

Hyperactive children suffer from a disorder that is both baffling and complex. Between 3 and 5 percent of the children in the United States may be involved. No one knows exactly why about ten times as many boys as girls are considered hyperactive.

Perhaps there is a hyperactive child in your neighborhood. If so, you may be familiar with the symptoms of a Fidgety Fred.

Fred's problems began to be especially noticeable when he was three years old, although some hyperactive children seem to be in constant motion from the time they are born. Fred was always very active, and when he was tall enough to unlatch doors, keeping him out of trouble was almost impossible. His actions involved a much wider area than when he was confined to his own house and outside play area. He would slip out of the house and run here and there, acting on impulse. One day, after a neighbor had cleaned out a closet full of spoiled canned food and thrown it in the trash pile behind her house, Fred discovered it and tossed each jar at the side of the house. Broken glass and spoiled food littered a wide area. One time he hit another child with a baseball bat, ran over some newly cemented sidewalk, and turned on the neighbor's hose. On another occasion, he disappeared when his mother turned her back for a moment. Frightened neighbors searched for hours before he was found under the bed in a house in the next block.

When Fred started nursery school, he was the only one in the class who could not lie still for a nap. Even when the teacher sat next to him for the entire period, he could not settle down the way the other children did. His restlessness caused problems in the classroom throughout his school years since he never followed through on any assigned task and had difficulty organizing his work. Teachers often sent him on errands or to the cafeteria, where the ladies preparing the lunch allowed him to help. He would flit from one place to another until someone sent him back to class. One of his teachers described Fred as a very lovable boy who was bright, but whose "motor was always running."

Doctors believe that hyperactivity is not really the cause of the problems of children described by this name. All these boys and girls have a severe inability to concentrate, and as a result, the American Psychiatric Association uses the term "attention deficiency disorder" to describe them. In recent years, the condition that is commonly called hyperactivity has also been described by names such as hyperkinetic, clumsy child syndrome, minimal brain dysfunction, and a long list of other terms. However, research has not uncovered the causes or the cure for this problem.

Some children appear to be helped to concentrate by the use of stimulant drugs, the opposite kind of medication that one might expect to be helpful. But the drugs have their drawbacks, such as interfering with sleep patterns and curbing appetite. The drugs may be misused, and in some cases may dull a child's senses. Since their introduction for hyperactive children in the 1930's, there have been many warnings about their use.

One widely publicized treatment for hyperactive children is the use of a special diet as prescribed originally by the allergist Dr. Benjamin Feingold. This diet eliminates food dyes, flavorings, and preservatives, leaving a diet composed mainly of the so-called natural foods. Although many parents are enthusiastic about this approach, some find that the diet eliminates most of the things that children enjoy eating and find it difficult to follow.

Some researchers believe hyperactivity is entirely physical, involving a deficiency of a chemical that conducts nerve impulses in the brain. Until more is known about the causes and treatment of this disorder, techniques such as quick rewards and punishment, consistent discipline, and the breaking of tasks into small units that a child can follow provide some help to distraught parents and teach-

31

ers. Some children outgrow their lack of ability to concentrate, but others continue to have problems in adult life.

Fire-setting by children is another kind of behavior that may or may not be due to emotional problems. Fires set by children between ages four and seven are usually just the result of curiosity and playing with matches to light small fires. Small fires may get out of control and often cause parents to feel that their children have set them deliberately. But deliberate fire-setting is a relatively rare occurrence, even among emotionally disturbed children.

Fire setters usually show a variety of other types of antisocial behavior, such as truancy and stealing. Many of these children are reported to have acute anxiety and frequent terrifying dreams and nightmares. When children set fires near their own homes, they may be trying to hurt someone in the family because they feel neglected or because they are trying to hurt those who are serious rivals for their parents' love.

Fires set by adolescents are usually more serious in nature than those set by younger children. The adolescent fire setter usually plans in advance and watches the fire with feelings of intense pleasure and excitement. The fire gives a sense of power, and this behavior is believed to be, as in the case of adult pyromaniacs, a displaced sexual expression.

Children who lie, steal, manipulate, destroy, and show no sense of guilt are often labeled as having character disorders. Phil is a high school student who shows many of the characteristics of a sociopath, as these people are sometimes called. He acts on impulse and lacks the capacity to plan ahead for any long period of time. In spite of his charming manners, he has few friends.

Phil really does not care about the feelings of other people unless he can use these individuals to his own advantage. Most people who know Phil thought he was a well-adjusted boy with no more than ordinary problems. They changed their opinion when it was discovered that he beat up a six-year-old child who had refused to move out of his way at a baseball game. Further examination revealed that he did not feel sorry about seriously injuring the child, although he pretended to, because he knew that this was expected of him.

Phil's parents had known for a long time that he tried to manipulate them, but they tried to protect him by covering his mistakes and by bailing him out whenever he was in trouble. Although they were upset by what Phil had done, they were relieved when they learned that social workers would be involved with Phil's case. His parents hoped that the workers would be able to provide some guidance for the whole family.

Mental health workers try to do what they can to reeducate unmanageable young people whose parents cannot control them, but this is a difficult problem. Many of these young people become involved with juvenile courts, although some, with help, grow out of their problems.

Children who have any of the problems described in this chapter are not out of touch with reality. Even when a child is known to have serious emotional problems, it is sometimes difficult to say exactly what is wrong with the child.

33

4
The World
of Autistic Children

Seven-year-old Evan sits on the floor in the corner of the room in his special school, rocking back and forth, hour after hour. He shows no interest in any living person other than himself, but parts of his own body seem to fascinate him. His head has been badly bruised because he is in the habit of banging it against the floor, an activity that sometimes lasts until he is forcibly stopped. Evan's vocabulary consists of a few words that do not make any sense, but yesterday he put a puzzle together. He did this with the blank side up, perhaps because he never notices the picture on the other side, which most children use as a guide. Perhaps he does not want to be exposed to anything that would tempt him to relate socially to the outside world. For some children, a retreat from the world is their only means of retaining some element of self. Evan has been diagnosed as retarded and autistic. Certainly, his behavior is strange.

Three-year-old Grace sits on the floor in the middle of the room with a large pad of paper in front of her. She is drawing circles, one after the other, and is seemingly content. When the teacher offers

Grace a new box of crayons, she ignores the offer. The teacher knows that if she tries to move close to Grace, she will kick, scratch and scream. Whenever Grace looks in the direction of the teacher, or toward any other person, she seems to look right through the person. She might just as well look at a blank wall, for there is never an expression of recognition on her face. She does not speak; she does not seem to hear.

Even when Grace was a tiny baby, she seemed to be developing much as other children do. She responded to her mother when she sang to her. She had even begun to say a few words, but, without warning, Grace changed when she reached the age of fourteen months. She no longer paid any attention to anyone around her. Nor did she learn to walk at an age when most children do. Grace is an autistic child, one who suffers from a disorder called infantile autism.

Infantile autism is a disabling mental disorder that affects from 5 to 15 of every 10,000 children. Some babies exhibit symptoms very early in their lives, while other children appear to be developing normally until sometime before the age of three, when symptoms appear. Many autistic children act as if they are deaf, but they become startled at a sudden burst of noise or notice the quiet crumpling of a candy wrapper, giving evidence that they really do hear. Autistic children have difficulty in relating to other people; they resist learning, and have no fear of real dangers. They may be greatly upset by a simple change in routine or the position of furniture. For example, George screamed in rage when anyone moved anything in his room. Even the changing of a light bulb would send him into a tantrum. This need for sameness may be a way of lessening anxiety, an effort to establish laws by which things happen.

Many autistic children indicate their needs by gestures. Cindy was a five-year-old child who never spoke. When she wanted a cookie, she might take her mother's arm and use it as a tool to reach the cookie on a plate. Then she would take the cookie from her mother's hand and eat it without appearing to notice that another person was involved in any way.

Inappropriate language often characterizes those autistic children who do speak. For example, when Steve was brushing his teeth, he had some difficulty getting the toothpaste out of the tube. He remarked, "What's the matter? Did your wagon get stuck?" Steve's mother recognized these questions as hers from the time Steve had been trying to pull his wagon around the garden and the wheels stuck on the exposed root of a tree. His comment about the wagon was not directed at anyone in particular, but it was used at a time when he was frustrated much as he had been when the wagon was stuck.

Jeff is an autistic child who often kicked the wall for hours on end. His mother threatened to take his shoes off once when he was kicking the wall at nap time. Some years later, when Jeff was scolded for flicking a light switch off and on, he responded, "Want me to take your shoes off?"

Many autistic children speak in reverse pronouns. For example, if one is told, "It is time for you to go to bed," the child may respond, "Time for you to go to bed," because there seems no way for him or her to rephrase the statement. Autistic children often echo back what is told to them, a trait that is known as echolalic speech. Phrases or much longer verbal expressions may be repeated immediately, exactly as they are said, or something may be repeated at a much later time. In the case of Steve, his mother estimated that six or seven years had passed after the actual incident with the wagon.

Some autistic children repeat long lists of things, such as a list of Presidents of the United States, or an entire television commercial, without showing any sign of understanding what they are saying.

Head-banging, inappropriate laughing and giggling, twirling and other strong physical overactivity are common characteristics of autism. Spinning objects and ongoing odd play activities are common. For example, Lisa would sit for hours feeling a necklace that was made of a chain and several beads.

Some autistic children bite themselves until they bleed, kick walls until they make holes in them, even though they hurt themselves, and mutilate themselves in other ways. When children begin this kind of behavior, parents, teachers, or other caretakers may have to hold them for as long as several hours. Telling such children that they are hurting themselves is meaningless; adult arms around the child's body offer protection.

Imagine living with a child who does not respond to cuddling, to words, or to attention. Autism varies in its severity, but many autistic children spin jar lids incessantly, or arrange objects in neat rows. Upsetting such a pattern may cause violent actions or intense crying. While rocking back and forth is typical for many normal children, autistic children use this behavior frequently and for extremely long periods of time.

Many autistic children scream day and night, while others remain passive in their cribs. In its mild form, autism resembles a learning disability, and many such children are labeled retarded, even though they are capable. Occasionally, an autistic child excels in one area, such as unusual musical ability, drawing, or feats of memory. Intelligence testing is very difficult and often impossible, because the child does not respond. In some cases, a child appears to be holding back because of fear. By not hearing, by not becoming involved, the child is safe from risk of failure. But flashes of intelligent behavior make a sharp contrast between what these children usually do and what they can do.

Diagnosis of autism is often difficult, since it depends entirely on observations of behavior. Although children who are not autistic may show some of the traits of autism, those who suffer from this disorder behave abnormally all the time. The National Society for Children and Adults with Autism suggests that any child who exhibits seven or more of the following behaviors and shows inappropriate behavior for his or her age continually should be given thorough medical and psychiatric examinations. The behaviors in their checklist are: has difficulty in mixing with other children; acts as if deaf, resists learning; shows no fear of real dangers; resists change in routine; indicates needs by gestures; laughs and giggles inappropriately; is not cuddly; shows marked physical overactivity; uses no eye contact; is inappropriately attached to objects; spins objects; sustains odd play; and has a standoffish manner.

No one really knows exactly what causes autism, but theories about possible causes have changed considerably. In the past, many parents were told that they did not treat their babies with enough emotional warmth. These "refrigerator parents," as they were called by professionals, were often parents who admitted they did not want their children in the first place. This was considered to have made them cold and rejecting. Mothers who were especially close to their autistic children were accused of being so overprotective that they denied them the right to demand. These children were thought to be emotionally fused with their mothers, making them withdraw from the real world.

Parents no longer need to suffer from the guilt that they felt when they were told their children were autistic because of their own actions. Whatever the causes of autism may be, they are not rejection, understimulation, or smothering attention. Many professionals suggest that it is the child's lack of responsiveness that makes a parent turn away from being close to the child. Living with a child who does not cuddle, who offers no emotional feedback, whose behavior is bizarre and even self-destructive, who cannot or will not follow directions, can certainly exact a great emotional toll on parents.

Most experts agree that no known factors in a child's psychological environment have been shown to cause autism. Chemical exposure or German measles during the mother's pregnancy, phenylketonuria and certain other genetic defects may be involved.

There is no known medical cure for all autistic children, but some recent experiences with a prescription drug, flenfluramine, which has been used to control the appetites of fat people, appear to provide some hope. About 40 percent of autistic children have higher than normal levels of the chemical serotonin, which may interfere with the functioning of brain cells. Researchers tried flenfluramine in an effort to reduce the concentration of serotonin. They caution that much more work must be done, but they are encouraged by the effects of this drug in stopping compulsive body movements and increasing sociability in a small number of cases.

Some therapists, and some parents who act as therapists for their children, have made progress in relating to them by using intense physical stimulation. Stroking, massaging, and forcing eye contact with children who struggle against accepting these actions has helped in some cases. Each child differs, but appropriate training tailored to each one's needs and skills has helped some autistic children to improve to the point where they can hold jobs that do not involve skill in social relationships.

Even professionals disagree about how to classify autistic behavior. Some call autism a psychosis, but not all autistic children are seriously emotionally disturbed. The United States Department of Education classifies them as "other health impaired" under the definition of handicapped children. Autistic children rarely develop delusions and hallucinations, and this separates autism from mental disorders which appear similar. Autism is not the same as mental retardation, although autistic children often seem to be functioning at a retarded level. It has been known to occur in children of all levels of intelligence. People who exhibit this kind of weird behavior are among those most in need of human help.

Suppose you know a child who suffers from autism. You have learned to help by putting your arms around him and holding him when he tries to hurt himself. You can relieve his parents for an hour or more at a time by watching him. Suppose he climbed to the second floor of the house and stepped out of an open window onto the porch roof. Would you panic? Or would you quickly call for help? Young people who have learned to work with autistic children play an important part in the lives of the families. Some of these young people find the experience so rewarding that they make a career of working with children who suffer from this disorder.

While autism is more common than muscular dystrophy and twice as common as congenital blindness, it is poorly understood. Much research is needed to find the causes of autism and ways to prevent and cure it.

5
Schizophrenia

Fifteen-year-old Mary is suffering from one of the most common and most serious of mental diseases: schizophrenia. She is an attractive girl, but she sometimes sees herself as having extra features on her face. She may believe that her nose has an extra part, making it longer than her whole head. Or she may believe that she has an eye in her forehead. Today, Mary believes that her hands have turned white and that they are numb. They are made of plaster, so she cannot move them. Suddenly, she sees a large number of hands floating around the room. Some of them drop and break into little pieces as they hit the floor, just as plaster would. There is a sense of doom in Mary when she hears voices calling from the lamp in the corner of the room. The voices tell her that she is fat and ugly and that she has been a bad girl. When she tries to tell the doctor how she feels, the words come out jumbled and the doctor has difficulty in understanding what Mary means. Mary looks at the doctor and wonders if he is really a man; sometimes she is not sure if she, herself, is male or female. Mary often has trouble concentrating, and her thoughts confuse her. Sometimes she giggles when she really feels sad, and sometimes she feels nothing at all, just a great emptiness.

After a few minutes, Mary, who is in the doctor's office, comes back to the real world. She is able to tell her doctor what she has just experienced, but many schizophrenics cannot relate their experiences to anyone even after they have just happened.

Schizophrenia is probably not a single disorder, but rather a group of complex, puzzling conditions. One of the puzzles involves diagnosis, for doctors may not agree about whether or not a person is really schizophrenic. The illness usually begins in adolescence or early adulthood. The relationship between childhood schizophrenia and adult schizophrenia is a subject of controversy. The childhood disorder may not be true schizophrenia; it may be a special type or it may represent an early or severe form of adult schizophrenia. Children who suffer from this disease do not necessarily grow up to be adult schizophrenics.

Some people talk about childhood schizophrenia and autism interchangeably, while others feel that there are children who are not schizophrenic but suffer from still a different kind of childhood disease. There are some definite differences between autism and other severe disorders such as a schizophrenia-like disease occurring during childhood. Autism is present from birth, while a schizophrenic child begins to show symptoms after the age of five. The autistic child shows no social interaction, while the nonautistic child is very dependent on one or more adults.

The incidence of childhood schizophrenia is believed to be higher than that of autism, ranging about 6 or 7 per 10,000 children. And the number of family members suffering from mental disorders is greater too. There is more chance that someone in your neighborhood is schizophrenic than autistic. It may be a child, a teenager, or the mother or father of one of your friends or neighbors. It is helpful to recognize the symptoms of this tragic disease. Although the disease is somewhat different for children than for adults, adolescent schizophrenics are treated in the same way as adults.

Imaginary situations and beliefs are common among schizophrenic children, but they are seldom observed in autistic children. For example, ten-year-old Gary believes that he is an automobile tire. Now and then he lies on the floor in a motionless heap, feeling that he is deflated. He remains there until someone "pumps him up." Betsy hears voices that tell her what to do. Joe thinks he has a little man in his stomach who tells him to do bad things. When Joe is asked to draw a picture of himself, he draws a boy with a little person in the area of his stomach. If asked, he will explain that that is the little man whose voices he hears. Susie believes that she is a mechanical doll. When she stops walking, she asks someone to wind her up. Then she continues for a time. Each morning, she stays still in her bed until the imagined key in her back is wound to give her energy.

There is disagreement about the relationship between childhood schizophrenia and adult schizophrenia. The childhood disorder may be a special type or it may represent an early or severe form of adult schizophrenia. Children who suffer from this disease do not necessarily grow up to be adult schizophrenics.

Although there are many types of schizophrenia, the symptoms frequently include delusions (beliefs that something imagined really exists), hallucinations (such as those experienced by Mary), and catatonia (staying in one position for a long time, or peculiar posturing or grimacing). One classic definition of schizophrenia is "disorganized personality." Another popular definition is "profound disturbance in relationship to the real world." This may be reflected in every aspect of a person's thinking and feeling.

Speech of a person suffering from schizophrenia follows a train of thought that may be impossible to follow. For example, a schizophrenic might say the following sentences in rapid succession: "My uncle gave me a big bag. I cannot go to the party. The elephant is outside." Doctors often refer to such speech as "word salad."

Schizophrenic behavior is typically inappropriate. For example, when a schizophrenic boy was told that his friend had died, he laughed and sang a song. Actually, the boy had always been devoted to his friend.

Extreme changes in decisions and behavior are common. A schizophrenic might describe an event in the following way: "I never had such a good time as I did at the dance. I never did like to dance, no wonder it was so awful. I loved the dance. The music was too loud. I'm glad they only played quiet music."

Many schizophrenics do not enjoy life the way

most people do. For example, they do not get satisfaction from a job well done, or derive pleasure from conversing with a friend, or enjoy other relationships with people that are an important part of everyday life.

Maintaining attention is another problem for schizophrenics. They are unable to focus their attention on a specific situation or concentrate on something. They appear to be responding to a multitude of stimuli at any one time.

A schizophrenic person often views the world differently from most people. Every person sees the world from his or her own point of view. One popular illustration of this point is the way four healthy people look at a trapeze show. One may be most interested in the danger and the risks involved when trapezists somersault in the air. Another person may note the sturdiness of the ropes and pulleys, while another may talk about the grace with which the act was performed. And the fourth person may be impressed with the attractiveness of the performers. The act might be viewed by a schizophrenic person in any of the above ways, or it may be viewed in a way that would seem very weird. He or she might see monkeys or cats swinging from the ropes, rather than the people who are really there.

People who are schizophrenic do not suffer from such symptoms all the time. Nor do all people suffer from all the symptoms. In fact, no two cases are alike. Even within one individual, the symptoms may vary from time to time.

When severe symptoms appear, the person is said to be suffering from acute schizophrenia, such as the attack described in the case of Mary at the

46

beginning of this chapter. Mary, or others who suffer from acute schizophrenia, may have only one episode, or she may have many during her lifetime. In between the episodes, she lives a relatively normal life. The symptoms may disappear entirely without treatment. Psychiatrists have found that the more acute the onset of an attack, the better the chances are for a complete recovery.

In the case of chronic schizophrenia, the patient requires continued care. The symptoms do not disappear entirely, and the patient is usually kept on medication to control the symptoms.

Schizophrenia has been called the greatest challenge of the researchers who are trying to learn about mental illness. This disorder has probably always troubled humankind. It was called *dementia praecox* in 1896, a name suggesting both progressive deterioration and early onset, since the disease commonly appears in adolescence. For years, this name was considered a diagnostic trash basket for any form of insanity that could not be understood. In 1911, Dr. Eugen Bleuler, a Swiss psychiatrist, coined the word "schizophrenia," but there is still some disagreement about which diseases should and should not be included under this label. Certainly, schizophrenics are not the Jekyll-and-Hyde split personalities that many people assign to them. In spite of many years of research, little is known about the causes of this disorder that, by some estimates, affects as many as 1 in 1,000 people. There are clues, however, that may bring about at least a partial solution to this puzzling disease or diseases.

Most researchers agree that schizophrenics can

not attend to tasks because many irrelevant or fleeting thoughts intrude. And they do agree that a combination of factors is probably responsible for schizophrenia. The disorder tends to run in families. The children of a schizophrenic parent have a 10 percent chance of developing it, and, in the case of identical twins, if one becomes schizophrenic, there is a 50 percent chance that the other twin will, too. With fraternal twins, the rate is only about 10 percent, the same as for other brothers and sisters. Studies with children of schizophrenic parents who have been adopted helped to demonstrate that a hereditary factor appears to be present in some types of the disorder. If the disease were 100 percent genetic, however, if one identical twin developed the disease, the percentage for the other would be 100 percent and not 50 percent. Obviously, there must be some environmental factors as well.

At one time there was a tendency to blame parents for unclear communication with children as a cause of disordered thinking, but it is not certain whether such problems of communication in a family are a *cause* or a *result* of schizophrenia.

Researchers continue to explore the possibility of a chemical defect in the bodies of schizophrenics, concentrating on the substances that carry impulses from one nerve to another. According to one theory, schizophrenics have an excess of the chemical dopamine in certain sites in the brain. The interest in this chemical has been triggered by the fact that certain drugs effective in treating symptoms of schizophrenia interfere with the action of dopamine. Other drugs, such as amphetamines, that

48

release dopamine, can create psychosis in normal individuals.

One theory is that schizophrenics are slow to process incoming information. The brain processes information in three steps: (1) initial contact with a piece of information; (2) storage of information in an unconscious "storage bin"; (3) transfer of the information to the conscious. Dr. David L. Braff of the University of California Medical Center, San Diego, and Dr. Dennis Saccuzzo of San Diego State University have shown that, in schizophrenics, the transfer of information from the storage bin to the conscious is slower than normal. Before one piece of information can be transferred from the storage bin, another piece of information enters, interfering with or erasing the first piece of information. This would make the pieces of information jumbled, explaining why schizophrenics suffer from abnormal perception, disorganized thinking, and confusion.

The structure of the brain has been another area of research. Two new kinds of brain scans are helping to provide leads. One is the CAT scan, which shows the brain's anatomy, and the other is the PET scan, which shows brain function and metabolism. There have been instances of abnormalities in specific parts of the brains of schizophrenic patients.

Chemical tests of the spinal fluid of schizophrenics suggest that a slow virus may be involved. If this is the case, there may be hope that a vaccine may someday be found that would prevent some types of this dread disease.

Several factors may combine to cause schizophrenia. Stress appears to play a part. In the case of identical twins, the baby who suffered most at birth is the one who is more likely to suffer from the disease.

Being disabled with schizophrenia is difficult to imagine. If a young person loses the ability to enjoy life, to relate to other people socially, to work, and has no energy for even the most normal of routines, what is left? Unfortunately, many schizophrenics suffer frightful experiences. A boy may be talking to his teacher while her face gradually appears to change. He sees her tongue grow longer and longer until it reaches below her neck. He is conscious of the fact that it is not really any larger than normal, still he sees the huge tongue. Another person in this class for young schizophrenics may have a voice that tells her to save the world by tearing all the papers to shreds. The voice begins as a strange buzzing noise, then it seems that her thoughts are being spoken aloud. Sometimes Mary feels that her own thoughts are leaving her body and are being transmitted to everyone else, so that everyone knows just what she is thinking. Her whole life seems to be coming apart and her brain is about ready to explode.

The horror of these feelings cannot be imagined by anyone who has not experienced them, but unfortunately the number of people who suffer from schizophrenia at some time in their lives is estimated to be as much as 2 percent of the population in the United States. Many so-called normal individuals experience some of the characteristics of schizophrenia briefly. Since there is so much disagreement about the diagnosis of schizophrenia, no wonder it is difficult to estimate the percentage of people who suffer from the disease. Psychiatrists in America are thought to apply the label more frequently than those in Europe. Since schizophrenia is not a single condition, it is not surprising to find a great deal of confusion about it.

Individuals vary greatly in their need for treatment. The discovery of the drug chlorpromazine in the 1950s ended the need for straitjackets. This drug and other new ones helped to empty the back wards of hospitals by bringing the most bizarre hallucinations and delusions under control. But these drugs do not "cure" schizophrenics. The inability to take an interest in the world outside themselves is still present, and, for many, the terror still lies beneath apparent apathy.

Studies show that about 25 percent of schizophrenics achieve full recovery, about 50 percent recover partially, and the other 25 percent require lifelong care. Even when people are considered cured, some scars remain. Just as a broken leg is not quite the same as it was before it was broken, a person who has suffered from schizophrenia has lived through a powerful experience that will have an effect on life in the future.

Can schizophrenia be prevented? One effort in this direction involves early diagnosis. Suppose your sister suddenly lost all interest in school, brought home terrible grades, and gave up seeing her friends. She tells you that one of the boys in her class is trying to run her life and has poisoned her friends against her. She sometimes forgets appointments. Now and then, she arrives at a place and does not know why she went. Then she goes home and asks someone in the family why she went. Some of these symptoms may sound like schizophrenia. But remember, even doctors have trouble making a diagnosis. You would know, for certain, that your sister needs professional help.

Scientists have made little progress toward identifying children who are likely to become schizophrenic, but some preliminary studies suggest that certain tests of brain activity may serve to predict the onset of adult schizophrenia. The goal of such tests and follow-up studies is to develop intervention for those who carry schizophrenic genes. If great strides can be made in genetic engineering, scientists hope that such genes might be altered. This is a very distant goal.

More definite and concrete help can come today through concern for people who are schizophrenic or who have shown some recovery. The fear that is felt by those around the patient is considered one of the greatest roadblocks to recovery that a schizophrenic faces. Society tends to keep such people at a distance rather than to supply the attention that would be most helpful to such a person. The universal fear of "losing my mind" causes difficulty for those who have problems relating to others.

Suppose a boy who is suffering from schizophrenia lives in your neighborhood. Would you feel uncomfortable about trying to make friends with him? Would you be willing to visit him, share something of yours with him even if there is a chance that it may not be returned?

There is an urgent and persistent need for more research to help answer questions about the causes, prevention, and treatment of schizophrenia.

6
Depression

Brian felt terrible for more than a month before his twelfth birthday. He had headaches and stomachaches, and he moped around much of the time. His mother said he had tired blood, and his father said it was growing pains. His doctor could not find anything physically wrong with him, but when Brian became withdrawn and his grades at school dropped, the doctor referred him to a psychiatrist, who made a diagnosis of depression.

Depression is a condition that is very different from just feeling blue for a few days. In severe cases, the emotional pain can be as great as the pain from cancer. It is difficult for people who have never suffered from this illness to appreciate how much it hurts. The complaints of a depressed person may seem exaggerated, but the pain is excruciating. Depressed people feel worthless. The anguish is so great that many of them have hurt themselves physically with the hope that the physical pain might take away the emotional pain. They often say, "I am so weak, I cannot do anything. I do not have the strength to lift a small chair." Or "My head is so heavy that I can't hold it up." They criticize themselves excessively, and they feel guilty about situations over which they have no control. They complain about life being empty and that there is nothing left to live for. In some cases, they take actions that lead to suicide.

One of the outstanding features of adult depression is a sense of hopelessness, especially following a loss. For many years, psychiatrists did not believe that children could suffer from depression. Since young children have a very limited ability to consider the future beyond the time directly ahead, how could they feel that the future was hopeless? Certainly, another year seems like an endless period of time for a young child. But there are symptoms other than hopelessness that indicate that children may be depressed.

Many experts have come to believe that childhood depression afflicts about 2 percent of all young children. Some researchers think depression may even be present in certain infants who have been separated from their mothers, but there is more agreement among experts that children over six may be depressed. According to Dr. Jamad Kashani, a child psychiatrist at the University of Missouri Medical School, there may be 400,000 depressed children in the United States. Other authorities suggest that depression in children may be far more common than this. A report from the National Institute of Mental Health concludes that as many as 1 in 5 children suffer from depression.

Teenage depression is more like the adult disorder than childhood depression is. In the United States, from 6 million to 14 million teenagers and adults are suffering from depression. These people lose the capacity for enjoying life, sleep too much or too little, lose their appetites, become upset by small things, are anxious, restless, or may have lost interest in everything. Many of them withdraw from friends and relatives. And all of them feel worthless. But other symptoms can mask depression, as in the case of Brian, who suffered from headaches and stomachaches. Often vague feelings of sickness interfere with normal living. If you think that you or someone in your family may be suffering from depression, it is wise to consult a concerned adult at home or school. A doctor will be able to help.

Mike is rather typical of a teenager who suffers from depresssion. He was an honor student, a soccer player, a boy who had everything. At least, it seemed that way to his parents before he began spending much of his time in his room alone. Mike's grades started to fall. He quit the soccer team, and he was moody. Some days he seemed to be getting himself organized again, but much of the time, he was angry with the world.

One day, Mike was starting to get dressed when he noticed that his dark-gray corduroys were full of lint. When he reached in his drawer for another pair of pants, he found that most of them were in the same condition. He let out a scream that could be heard all over the house.

Mike's mother had noticed other instances of his strange behavior for some time. When a friend in whom she confided suggested that Mike might be suffering from depression, his mother could not agree. She argued that he was not particularly sad, just different. She explained that he disobeys, he does not eat properly, he sleeps at odd times during the day and stays up all night on weekends, and he is angry much of the time. Can this be depression?

Mike's father decided that he was going through a phase. "Just the usual adolescent rebellion," he said. "Mike will be fine after this stage passes."

No one had really listened to Mike when he tried to explain how lost he felt when his best friend moved to another city. Nor did they notice how much he missed his cat. The cat was old and his parents had remarked that it was time for the cat to die. They did not realize that Mike had talked to the cat each night in his room, sharing his experiences with her.

Mike's behavior grew worse. He felt frightened when he began discovering that his parents were not as perfect as he had once believed them to be. No one explained to him that this was a natural part of breaking away from his parents and becoming independent. Physical changes in Mike's body made him feel awkward. He felt overwhelmed by all the changes that are a natural part of adolescence. Mike's self-esteem was so shaky that he withdrew from his peers even though he desperately wanted to be part of the crowd. Each correction by a parent or teacher caused him to react intensely. He had no way of knowing that this difficult time would pass, and he felt both helpless and hopeless.

Mike became so rebellious that his parents consulted a therapist about his behavior. They found it hard to believe that most teenagers suffer from some degree of depression. For Mike, this was a severe depression.

"This is the best time of their lives," his father

insisted. Actually, he had forgotten the difficult times during his own early years. "Why should Mike be depressed when he has everything anyone could want?"

When asked if Mike had suffered any recent losses, one of the triggers in a severe adult depression, Mike's parents mentioned that his cat had died and that his closest friend had moved. But, they insisted, Mike had not shown any signs of sadness about either loss. How could he be depressed?

The therapist explained that many young people cannot express their sadness. Their "cry for help" is diguised by rebellion, destructive behavior, and other actions that actually mask their depression.

Although adolescent depression is often self-limiting, there are ways to help a depressed person recover more rapidly. Many of these are very different from what seems the natural thing to do. For example, Mike's father kept telling him to cheer up. There were times when he felt Mike's depression was a result of willfulness, but when he accused Mike of this, the result was frustration for both of them.

Over a period of time, the therapist helped Mike and his parents to communicate better together. Mike began to take more control of his life and explore new interests. Gradually, he felt that he was going to be able to cope with the future and take care of himself.

If you have a friend or a relative who is depressed, you may be helpful.

Telling depressed people to "buck up" is not helpful. They cannot overcome their problems this way.

Reassuring depressed people that things will get better should be repeated many times. Even though they say they do not believe you, hearing this can help to overcome the feelings that things will never change.

Encourage a depressed person to do anything that he or she feels able to do. Activity helps. Running has been found to be especially beneficial.

Rather than inquiring what a depressed person would like to do, make suggestions, probing for a spark of interest. If you ask, "Would you like to go to a baseball game, a tennis match, a bingo game, or whatever?" you will probably get a negative answer. A more indirect route may work. Strike up a conversation about general topics and try to hit on something that engages the person's attention. If you can find some spark of interest, you can know you have helped. Sometimes, false statements about a subject with which the depressed person is familiar can spark him or her to correct you and take an interest.

Encourage, be kind, but do not try to force. If you try to make a depressed person do something, you may only cause him or her to feel guilty for not being able to respond.

Understand that depressed people have trouble making decisions and often exhibit poor judgment. Depressed people look frantically for ways out of their despair and can insist that taking certain major steps will help them. A boy who insists that changing schools will be the answer to overcoming his depression may, at a later date, blame his family for letting him do such a thing when he was depressed. Remember that depression is an illness, that feelings are out of kilter, and that serious decisions should not be made by a depressed person.

Take suicide threats seriously. Most people who are considering suicide give warning signals, such as putting unfinished business in order, giving away their possessions, expressing hopelessness, talking about suicide, or saying the world would be better off without him or her. When signals are present, do not leave the person alone. Arrange to get professional help quickly.

Most depressed people get well faster when they have good treatment. If someone in your family is suffering from depression, you can help by recognizing that this illness affects the person's behavior. He or she is not weird because of spite, meanness, or willfulness. Whether the depression comes from chemical changes within or from too much stress in the environment, patience and the understanding of family and friends is an important help toward making that person better. However, you should not blame yourself or the depressed person if your efforts do not seem to help. There are many cases where nothing seems to make a difference, so friends and family should not feel guilty or make heroic efforts. Ask a professional counselor if there is something you can do, and have patience.

7
Anorexia Nervosa and Other Eating Disorders

When Jane was twelve years old, she was five feet tall and weighed 140 pounds. Jane claimed that her mother nagged at every meal about how much food she ate. Jane was tired of hearing about it. Actually, she really did not like the way she looked; she didn't even like herself. Her mother and father were both very careful about their weight and they both dressed to perfection. Jane, on the other hand, was sloppy about her appearance. "Why bother to clothe a fat slob?" was a remark her mother had made to a friend.

A big party was planned for Jane's sister's engagement to a man who treated Jane with respect in spite of her weight. Jane wanted to please him and to look nice for the party, so she made up her mind to lose weight. First, she bought a calorie counter then she allowed herself 900 calories a day. At first the hunger was awful, but Jane stuck to her diet.

When Jane reached 100 pounds, she felt much better about herself and was able to deny any feelings of hunger. By the time she wore a size 5 dress, Jane thoroughly enjoyed the many compliments from her family and friends. She felt so great that she decided to continue with her diet. She began shaving calories from her original diet plan until she was down to 300 calories a day. The weight was really coming off. When she sat at the dinner table, she chewed on some food, then hid it in her napkin. Jane's parents prodded her to eat more so she would gain some weight, but she paid no attention. She felt good about being in complete control of herself.

Jane had always tried very hard to obey her family, even when she was overweight and was unable to control her diet. She continued to do exactly what they said, never questioning their orders and never getting angry. But Jane had her secret. Jane's parents took pride in telling their friends that their daughter never did anything without consulting them, but her continued weight loss began to be a matter of great concern.

When Jane's sister was married, Jane attracted much attention because she was so very thin. Although everyone had complimented her about the weight she had lost, now they suggested that it was time to try to gain some weight. However, Jane continued to see herself as fat and continued to diet.

Jane suffered from a disease known as anorexia nervosa. This is a dangerous, devastating form of illness that is considered epidemic among girls in their teens. In the case of anorexia nervosa, individuals think that they are fat when they are really quite thin. Victims deny that they have a problem. No matter how often people tell them that they look just fine the way they are, they think they need to lose more weight. They continue dieting with such determination that treatment is either difficult or impossible. New research suggests that the behavior problem may lead to a chemical disorder in the body which may push the dieter to the point of starvation. Unfortunately, as many as 10 to 15 percent of anorexics actually starve to death.

Anorexia nervosa commonly begins after a period of the kind of dieting that is usual among teenage girls, but the weight loss continues well beyond the point that most people consider attractive. The problem exists mainly among young girls in their teens, affecting about 1 in 250 girls. According to some estimates, the rate is as high as 1 in 100. Fewer than 10 percent of the cases involve boys.

Anorexia is an emotional disorder that is complicated by the fact that the body is deprived of the food it needs. Some anorexics eat as little as just one egg a day. Most of these girls lose about 20 percent to 25 percent of their body weight, have a low pulse rate, are excessively constipated, are depressed, lack menstrual periods, are hyperactive, and have low blood pressure and a distorted body image. Anorexics suffer from low body temperature so they feel cold most of the time. Some grow fine hair all over their bodies.

Although the person suffering from anorexia nervosa is obsessed with food, she does not eat because of emotional problems. Many anorexics have felt ineffective, empty, worthless, and out of control until they are in control of their own bodies. Then they also may feel in control of many factors in their environment. Jane's parents could not control her body, and her refusal of food was a way of rebelling against them. Sometimes anorexia is used as rebellion against school and against growing up. Many of the girls who develop this disease were dependable overachievers who seldom caused any trouble for their families. Excessive dieting can make them the focus of family attention and give them a sense of mastery over themselves and others.

The sooner the problem of anorexia is recognized, the easier it is to intercept it. Some early signs include social isolation, strange eating habits, such as cutting food into tiny pieces and avoiding many meals. Extreme weight loss is considered a rather late symptom of the disease.

Anorexics can recover without treatment and force feeding in the hospital, but many do continue in ill health for a long period of time or even die from this illness. Length of treatment varies from about ten sessions with a therapist to two or three years. The type of family therapy that is used at the Philadelphia Child Guidance Center lasts about six months with an 85 percent rate of cure. In this type of therapy, the focus is on changing patterns of family interaction. There are a number of different kinds of therapy in use throughout the United States, and their particular effectiveness depends somewhat on the individual patient. Sometimes the condition is just arrested and not really cured, even though there is a temporary weight gain. Relaxation techniques and careful nutritional programs help many anorexics, but they are no substitute for therapy.

Julie, an anorexic, discovered the binge-purge syndrome after she went through a very stressful time. Her mother had been sick, her married sister had lost her infant son, and Julie was worrying about college entrance examinations. She gave in to family pressure and began to eat more. After a few sizable meals, she went on an eating binge, stuffing herself with large amounts of food. But she was very concerned about the weight she was gaining and she had an uncomfortable feeling after each eating bout. One evening after a particularly large dinner, she felt she had to get rid of the spinach covered with cheese, the potatoes, the rolls and butter, and the pie and cheese she ate for dessert. So Julie went to the bathroom and threw up all the food she had just eaten. Suddenly, she had a wonderful feeling. She could eat and not gain weight. She could stop the family's nagging and still be in control. Julie had discovered bulimia.

Julie and hundreds of thousands of other young women, and a much smaller number of young men, share a condition in which they indulge in binge eating and follow this behavior by self-induced vomiting or purge by laxatives and diuretics (medicines that increase the excretions of liquids from the body). No one knows how many people suffer from bulimia, but it is estimated that there are at least 500,000 in the United States and probably a million use this technique in their relentless pursuit of thinness.

There is some disagreement about whether anorexia nervosa and bulimia are separate disorders or whether they are two phases of the same disorder and should be called bulimarexia. No matter what the name, it is an extremely painful and disabling disorder.

When Julie discovered that she could eat and get rid of her food on command, she began using this technique frequently. Sometimes she would gorge on candy bars, throw them up, and eat some more. Of course, the fact that she could not wait for a

64

convenient time to get rid of her food limited her social life. She became so concerned with her secret that she had no time to spend with friends. She always had to make excuses about leaving the table immediately after a meal. It was a relief to have her own apartment when she started college. Now she could continue the binge-purge pattern without anyone suspecting. But Julie was not at all happy about her life. She was in control, but she was addicted to a pattern that did not allow her to participate in any of the usual activities. Even when she tried going out to dinner with anyone, she had a problem. The food obsession dominated her life.

According to Dr. Joel Yager, Director of the Eating Disorder Clinic at the University of California's Neuropsychiatric Institute, many people fall into one habit or another to relieve tension or anxiety. Such people drink, smoke, take various kinds of drugs, become exercise buffs, medicate themselves with tranquilizers—they do what they have to do to help relieve their inner tensions. A growing number of people are using bulimic behavior the same way. For some people it becomes an absorbing way of life.

Dr. Yager says that bulimics feel enslaved by their compulsion, as though it had a life and power of its own. It becomes a focused attention that serves the sufferer as a totally compelling distraction, which in an odd way sustains them. "Their private emotional life becomes so dominated by food that they think of nothing else. They are completely absorbed in the process of eating and purging, and there is little time for other problems."

Many of the individuals who resort to anorexia

nervosa, bulimia, or bulimarexia are frightened, lonely, and unfulfilled. They are perfectionists who may be suffering from depression before they develop the eating disorder or they may develop the eating disorder because they are depressed. In any case, the consequences can be devastating. In addition to those medical problems that come with anorexia, there can be damage to the esophagus from excessive vomiting, and damage to the anus from the use of laxatives. The body loses chemicals that it needs, such as sodium, potassium, and calcium, and the teeth decay from the constant bathing of stomach acid during vomiting. Overstimulation of the salivary glands may cause a condition known as "squirrel face" in which the person's cheeks are full and round. Occasionally, intense bouts of vomiting tear the wall of the stomach or esophagus and cause hemorrhaging. Obviously, bulimia is a very serious condition, not just a little game that many girls consider their special secret.

Awareness of the fact that anorexia nervosa and bulimia are eating disorders shared by many others helps sufferers to seek help. Treatment is tailored to each individual, but there are still many puzzles connected with these eating disorders. Self-help groups, private and group therapy, and behavior modification are some of the methods used as treatment. Since the physical results can be quite serious, researchers, clinicians, and educators are searching for better ways of helping sufferers. Some of the organizations and books listed at the end of this book may be helpful to anorexics, bulimics, their families, and their friends.

8
Weird,
but Dangerous?

Suppose the headlines in your local newspaper inform you that 100 mentally ill patients are being discharged from the state hospital and being placed in special homes in the community or in their own apartments. Would you feel comfortable if such a home or apartment house happened to be near yours? Many people become upset at the idea of having mentally disturbed individuals as neighbors, because they feel that these people might be weird and dangerous. Most of those who object have never known anyone who has been in a mental hospital, nor have they ever visited a state hospital, so that they have some very mistaken ideas about the mentally ill people who might be living in the community.

Consider the case of Robbie, a fifteen-year-old boy who had been at the state hospital for four years. Robbie's parents were both retarded, and they did not know how to care for their children properly. His father was often gone from the home, and even when he was there, he paid little attention to the children. Sometimes he yelled at them or hit them when they did not behave the way he thought they should. Robbie's mother was never able to make the children listen to her, so she allowed them to do as they pleased. Like Robbie's father, she gave them little attention or love, but occasionally she would do odd things like tickling one of the children until he or she screamed or tore away from her.

When Robbie was a baby, he was hospitalized twice for malnutrition. At age four, Robbie was placed in a foster home because of his parents' neglect. By the time he was seven years old, Robbie was sent to an institution for the retarded. His development was so slow that psychologists believed he must be retarded. This overactive boy could not concentrate on anything, did not get along with other children, and was unable to behave or learn at school. Anyone who watched him could see that he acted like a child much younger than his years. Since none of the foster parents who tried to help him could manage to live with him, an institution seemed the only answer.

Robbie actually grew worse in the institution and the staff could not manage him. So the staff at the institution for the retarded sent Robbie to the state hospital because of his behavior problems. At the hospital, Robbie's behavior improved with therapy and encouragement. He went to school and was able to concentrate and enjoy learning. He made great progress, and when his IQ was tested after two years at the hospital, it was discovered that his intelligence was about average. Robbie was not really retarded, although he had been labeled that way for years. He had been neglected, mistreated, and deprived of a normal family life, so he never learned and developed as he should have. In addition to these problems, Robbie had a very low opinion of himself. From early in his childhood, he felt that no one really liked him or wanted him, so he must be very bad and undesirable.

Even though Robbie improved, he still had some problems in behaving appropriately. Since Robbie had spent so many years in institutions, he never learned the thousands of things that most people learn when they are exposed to the experiences of everyday life. He learned some inappropriate behavior from some of the more emotionally disturbed patients at the state hospital. Sometimes he misbehaved to get special attention. The psychologists and the psychiatrists who were treating Robbie realized that he would not be able to learn and develop further unless he could leave the hospital and learn normal ways of behaving from living and going to school in a more normal environment.

Robbie was one of the mentally ill patients that the newspaper article referred to, but he was certainly not dangerous. Even the behavior that seemed weird to many people was learned in an environment where that kind of behavior was normal.

Fortunately, Robbie went to live with a foster family who gave him love and understanding. He finished a vocational program at the local high school and now he is working as a janitor. Robbie has friends and hobbies and enjoys his life.

Mrs. Jones is an elderly, gray-haired, neatly dressed lady who enjoys reading, knitting, and watching the soap operas on television at the state hospital. She is friendly and polite to everyone, takes care of her own needs, and even helps the other patients make their beds. She chats about the latest news and complains that her roommate is very forgetful. Mrs. Jones appears quite normal and ordinary, Why, then, is she in the state hospital?

If you chatted with Mrs. Jones for a while, she would probably tell you that the doctors insist that the pain in her stomach is caused by an ulcer, but she knows better. Mrs. Jones insists that there are snakes in her belly that grew there after she had a flu shot containing snake eggs. No amount of persuasion, arguing, or scientific explanation can convince her that she is wrong.

Before Mrs. Jones came to the hospital, she had been living alone in an apartment next door to her sister. She had been able to care for herself, doing the shopping, cooking, and cleaning with only occasional assistance from her sister. She did not have many friends and she did not go out often; she preferred to spend most of her time at home. Mrs. Jones insisted that the snakes had been in her body for many years, but she was able to ignore them. When the pain she believed they caused was severe, she went to her doctor for help. He assured her that the medicine he gave her (a mild tranquilizer) would help her and it did.

About a month before Mrs. Jones was admitted to the state hospital, her sister died. At that time, Mrs. Jones began to worry more about the snakes. She experimented with different kinds of medicines that she had saved from earlier illnesses and she tried to drink a strong detergent diluted with water in an effort to kill the snakes. Then she stopped eating, thinking that she could starve the snakes to death. When she called her family doctor, he became worried about her health, and he sent her to the hospital.

It was clear that Mrs. Jones was mentally ill. She had a fixed delusion about the snakes, and her thinking was certainly illogical. Although she harbored this delusion for many years, she had been able to live by herself with only a small amount of help from others. When her sister died, the loss became so stressful to her that she became more anxious and obsessed about the snakes, and her judgment deteriorated. She did not realize that she was actually harming herself by trying to get rid of the snakes.

In the hospital, Mrs. Jones received medication to reduce her anxiety. This stopped her from spending so much time thinking about the snakes. She also received emotional support from the staff and other patients, so she no longer felt afraid and lonely. Although she never was able to free herself entirely from the idea that she had snakes in her belly, she stopped trying to get rid of them.

Mrs. Jones is another patient who returned to the community when she improved in the hospital. She lives in her own apartment again. Once a week, she visits the community mental health center and the senior citizens center. Overall, she manages quite well. She has a few weird ideas, but she certainly is not dangerous.

Cases like those of Robbie and Mrs. Jones do not make the headlines. Many, many people who are mentally ill are no more dangerous than your best friend, your parents, or your favorite neighbor. Studies have shown that, in general, the mentally ill are no more dangerous than the population at large, and it is possible that they are less dangerous. However, when one reads the newspaper and finds that a man has brutally murdered a young boy, or someone has put poison in capsules of medicine and returned them to the drugstore shelves, it is easy to believe that there are many weird, sick, and dangerous people around. "They should all be locked up," is a common reaction after reports of strange and harmful behavior. Psychiatrists admit that they cannot predict future violent behavior with any degree of certainty.

Reports of mass murderers spread fear of all mentally ill persons. Consider the case of "Son of Sam," David Berkowitz, who terrorized many in the city of New York with his brutal actions. Berkowitz was arrested in August of 1977 after a year in which he killed six people and wounded seven others. He claimed that the killings were ordered by demons who spoke to him through the voices of barking dogs. Although two psychiatrists who examined Berkowitz believed his story, Dr. David Abrahamsen, an author and psychiatrist, did not. Dr. Abrahamsen believed that the man had created his demons as an alibi for the murders. In the case of a psychosis, hallucinations cannot be turned off and on at the will of the person, but in this case, Berkowitz seemed to be in control of the voices of the demons rather than being in their control. After many interviews, it was determined that Berkowitz was competent to stand trial. He was found guilty and sentenced to a string of twenty-five-year to life terms. After being sent to prison, Berkowitz himself called a press conference to announce that he had invented the story of the demons as an excuse for his murders. Even though the doctors disagreed about his mental illness, they agreed in general that this man was dangerous and probably would continue to be so.

Highly publicized murder trials focus attention on the problem of whether or not a person is capable of determining right from wrong. The legal profession asks if the accused was insane at the time of the crime. But there is no medical definition for "insane," and doctors attempt, instead, to determine whether or not the person was "psychotic," or out of touch with reality. Although the insanity plea is invoked in only about one of every thousand cases, it seems more common because the cases in which it is used tend to be sensational. When the insanity plea is used, however, it usually causes much controversy.

One of the most famous cases of disagreement about the mentally ill and dangerous person was the case of John W. Hinckley, Jr., who attempted to assassinate President Ronald Reagan on March 30, 1981. Hundreds of pages of testimony were recorded at the Hinckley trial. Some psychiatrists insisted that John Hinckley suffered from schizophrenia and was out of touch with reality, while others insisted that he was "sane" when he attempted to shoot the President. Dr. Park E. Dietz, a prosecution psychiatrist, insisted that Hinckley was suffering from four different relatively minor and common mental disorders. The decision of the jury, "not guilty by reason of insanity," caused much controversy and was said to have put the insanity defense itself on trial.

Before 1972, the criminally insane were usually held for life in mental institutions. In that year, the Supreme Court ruled that defendants who were incompetent to stand trial because of their mental illness could not be locked up indefinitely. This and a series of other rulings on the rights of mental patients have made it common for a person to be declared cured and released after eighteen months. A person may be released after six months if an appeal results in the finding that he or she no longer seems dangerous to society. Each case is decided individually and there are very definite criteria that must be met before a patient is released. However, it is not always possible to predict future behavior accurately, and there are some cases in which there have been tragic consequences.

Controversy continues about whether or not people who are found insane at the time of their crime should be forced to serve out long prison terms after they are no longer considered disturbed. In the past decade, new laws have been passed in some states in an effort to prevent abuses of the insanity defense. And experts are seeking ways of predicting whether persons are apt to be dangerous to society or themselves if released from an institution. When psychiatrists predict wrongly, the results can be tragic indeed for those who are confined unnecessarily as well as for those who are the victims of terrible crimes by former mental health patients.

In recent studies of violent juveniles, one of the most important factors that contributed to dangerous acts was the combination of some mental illness with witnessing or being the victim of extreme violence in the home. In the search for ways to prevent violence, the prevention of child abuse rates high on the list of objectives.

Certainly, many people may seem crazy to those around them, but only a very small percentage are dangerous. At the same time, psychiatrists claim that everyone is at least a bit crazy in some respects. There have been Presidents, musicians, artists, authors, politicians, and leaders in many fields who have, at times, exhibited very strange behavior. Being emotionally disturbed at some time does not mean that one will always be disturbed. The weirdness that is part of all of us waxes and wanes. Searching for the causes and the symptoms of mental disorders is a lifetime pursuit for health specialists. But helping the young person who acts "crazy" can benefit both the disturbed one and the helper, who may well be another child.

Mental Health Terms

AFFECT   An immediately expressed or observed emotion. An observable feeling. Common examples of affect are anger and sadness.

ANOREXIA NERVOSA   An inability to eat that lasts over a long period of time. Anorexics often see themselves as fat when they are really painfully thin.

ANXIETY   A feeling of tension, apprehension, or uneasiness. It may be focused on a situation, object, or activity that is avoided, or it may be free-floating, that is, not related to an identifiable cause.

AUTISM   An inability to relate to other people and a lack of response at attempts of others to communicate. Preoccupation with objects, mutism, echolalia, self-injury, and repetitive behavior may be displayed.

BULIMIA   Episodic binge eating accompanied by an awareness that eating patterns are abnormal. There may be frequent weight fluctuations because of alternating binges and fasting. Eating episodes may be terminated by self-induced vomiting, abdominal pain, or sleep. Depressed mood follows eating binges.

CATATONIC BEHAVIOR Bizarre physical behavior taking a variety of forms, such as: excited movements that appear purposeless; resistance to all instructions or attempts to be moved, or behavior that is opposite to instructions, such as clenching a jaw when asked to open the mouth; maintaining a rigid posture; holding a strange posture for a long period of time; stupor; waxy flexibility, such as allowing an arm or a leg to be "molded" into position as if it were made of pliable wax.

CHILDHOOD PSYCHOSIS Childhood behavior characterized by some of the following: lack of self-awareness, abnormal thought processes, inability to determine real from unreal, inappropriate display of feelings.

DELUSION A false personal belief, firmly sustained in spite of what is generally believed and in spite of obvious proof or evidence to the contrary. When the belief involves a value judgment, it is considered a delusion only if it is extreme. For example, a girl who thinks she is fat when she is slightly underweight would not be considered as suffering from a delusion. However, one with anorexia nervosa who was dangerously underweight but insisted she was fat would be considered delusional.

DEMENTIA PRAECOX An obsolete term for schizophrenia.

DEPRESSION A disorder of mood characterized by feelings of sadness, feelings of worthlessness and guilt, gloomy thoughts, loss of interest and pleasure in usual activities, loss of energy, insomnia, and lessened motor activity. There may be recurrent thoughts of death or suicide. True depression differs from temporary feelings of sadness.

ECHOLALIA   A person's automatic repetition, or echoing, of the exact words spoken to him or her.

ENCOPRESIS   A psychological condition in which there is voluntary or involuntary passing of solid waste matter in inappropriate places.

ENURESIS   A condition in which there is lack of control over the bladder and the passage of urine, not caused by physical disorder. Bed-wetting is more common, but enuresis may occur during the day as well. Enuresis is not necessarily a symptom of mental illness.

EXORCISM   The casting out of devils, demons, or devil spirits as practiced in ceremonies and rituals.

FAMILY THERAPY   A form of psychotherapy in which the entire family unit is involved as opposed to the treatment of only the individual who seems to be most troubled.

GROUP THERAPY   Any of a variety of treatment methods that involve a therapist and several other people.

HALLUCINATION   A phenomenon in which a person experiences sensations that have not been stimulated by real cues. Hallucinations may be auditory, visual, olfactory, or tactile, but the most common are auditory (hearing voices) or visual (seeing people or things that do not exist).

HYPERACTIVE CHILD   One who often fails to finish tasks that are started, does not seem to listen, is easily distracted, has difficulty concentrating on schoolwork or other tasks requiring sustained attention.

HYPERACTIVITY   Excessive activity.

HYPOACTIVITY   Below normal activity.

INSANE   A legal term applied to people who are judged not to be responsible for their actions because they cannot recognize their actions are criminal or do not realize what they are doing.

MADNESS   A nontechnical term used to describe some forms of mental illness. The term is now considered both vague and old-fashioned.

MANIC-DEPRESSIVE ILLNESS (BIPOLAR DISOR-DER)   A mood disorder characterized by periodic episodes of intense elation and physical activity and periods of intense depression, with normal periods in between. Some people alternate between the two mood extremes, while others experience only manic episodes. Most of these individuals eventually suffer a depressive episode. The elevated mood can be cheerful, high, euphoric, expansive. There may be increased irritability. Symptoms commonly include hyperactivity, inflated self-esteem, decreased need for sleep, pressure of speech, flight of ideas (continuous flow of fast speech with sudden changes from topic to topic).

MEGALOMANIA   A delusion that one is a person of great importance or fame.

MENTAL DISORDER   A severe psychological or behavioral condition with painful symptoms, and/or impairment of functioning.

MUTISM   The inability to speak, due to physical or psychological causes.

NARCISSISM   Self-love; preoccupation with self; ego-centrism.

OBSESSION   An idea, thought, or impulse that recurs persistently, is unwantd, and may be irrational, but is beyond the individual's control.

PARANOID PERSONALITY   A disorder characterized by suspiciousness, jealousy, hypersensitivity, rigidity. The individual shows a pattern of placing the blame for social failures on other people. Gross misinterpretation of external reality.

PSYCHOSIS   The term is often used to describe conditions showing severe disorganization of behavior and speech, as in the case of someone with advanced senility or a schizophrenic convinced that his or her delusions and hallucinations are real.

REMISSION   Recovery or significant improvement following an illness. This may be due to treatment or may just happen. It may be temporary or permanent.

SCHIZOPHRENIA   A group of disorders involving thought disturbance, hallucinations, or delusions. The disturbances affect both content and form of thought, perception, affect, relationship to the outside world, behavior, and sense of self. Bizarre delusions may be present, such as being controlled by an outside force, or having one's thoughts broadcasted. The person may suffer from delusions of persecution, thinking others are against him or her. Hallucinations are also characteristic, the most common being auditory. Often the individual hears voices giving commands or making comments about thoughts or behavior. Thinking may be extremely illogical, and links between ideas may be incomprehensible. Sometimes speech is incoherent as a result. Affect is sometimes totally bland or "flat" and the person seems without emotion. Sometimes affect is inappropriate.

WORD SALAD   Jumbles of words; sometimes noted in schizophrenia when thinking is very disorganized.

Suggestions
for Further Reading

Axline, Virginia M. *Dibs: In Search of Self.* Houghton Mifflin Co., 1964.

Bernheim, Kayla F.; Lewine, Richard R. J.; and Beale, Caroline T. *The Caring Family: Living with Chronic Mental Illness.* Random House, 1982.

Bruch, Hilde. *The Golden Cage: The Enigma of Anorexia Nervosa.* Harvard University Press, 1978.

D'Ambrosio, Richard. *No Language But a Cry.* Dell Publishing Co., 1971.

Freed, Alvyn M. *T.A. for Teens (and Other Important People).* Jalmar Press, 1976.

Friedrich, Otto. *Going Crazy: An Inquiry Into Madness in Our Time.* Simon & Schuster, 1976.

Green, Hannah. *I Never Promised You a Rose Garden.* Holt, Rinehart & Winston, 1964.

Greenfeld, Josh. *A Child Called Noah.* Holt, Rinehart & Winston, 1972.

Hyde, Margaret O. *Cry Softly! The Story of Child Abuse.* Westminster Press, 1980.

_____. *My Friend Wants to Run Away.* McGraw-Hill Book Co., 1979.

Hyde, Margaret O., and Forsyth, Elizabeth H. *Suicide: The Hidden Epidemic.* Franklin Watts, 1978.

Levenkron, Steven. *The Best Little Girl in the World.* Warner Books, 1979.

_____. *Treating and Overcoming Anorexia Nervosa.* Charles Scribner's Sons, 1982.

Minshull, Evelyn. *The Steps to My Best Friend's House.* Westminster Press, 1980.

Neufeld, John. *Lisa, Bright and Dark.* S. G. Phillips, 1969.

Palmer, R. L. *Anorexia Nervosa.* Penguin Books, 1981.

Park, Clara Claiborne. *The Siege: The First Eight Years of an Autistic Child.* Harcourt, Brace and World, 1967.

_____. *The Siege: The First Eight Years of an Autistic Child, With an Epilogue, Fifteen Years Later.* Atlantic Monthly Press, 1982.

Platt, Kin. *The Boy Who Could Make Himself Disappear.* Chilton Book Co., 1971.

Rothenberg, Mira. *Children with Emerald Eyes: Histories of Extraordinary Boys and Girls.* Dial Press, 1977.

Rubin, Theodore Isaac. *Jordi, together with Lisa and David.* Ballantine Books, 1962.

Sheehan, Susan. *Is There No Place on Earth for Me?* Houghton Mifflin Co., 1982.

Simon, Nissa. *Don't Worry, You're Normal: A Teenager's Guide to Self-Health.* Lippincott & Crowell, 1982.

Snyder, Solomon H. *The Troubled Mind: A Guide to Release from Distress.* McGraw-Hill Book Co., 1976.

For Further Information

American Anorexia Nervosa Association
133 Cedar Lane
Teaneck, NJ 07666

American Schizophrenic Association
56 West 45th Street
New York, NY 10036

American Schizophrenic Foundation
1114 First Avenue
New York, NY 10021

Center for Studies of Schizophrenia
National Institute of Mental Health
5600 Fishers Lane, Room 10-95
Rockville, MD 20852

Family Services of America
44 East 23rd Street
New York, NY 10010

National Association for Mental Health
1800 North Kent Street
Roslyn, VA 22209
   Chapters in state capitals and in many large cities.

National Association of Anorexia and Associated Disorders
Box 271
Highland Park, IL 60035

National Institute of Mental Health
Public Inquiries Room 9C-05
5600 Fishers Lane
Rockville, MD 20852

National Society for Children and Adults with Autism
Suite 1017
1234 Massachusetts Avenue, N.W.
Washington, DC 20005

Recovery, Inc.
116 South Michigan Avenue
Chicago, IL 60603

Adolescent Clinics in the United States and Canada

The following list is used by permission of the Society for Adolescent Medicine.

ALABAMA
Adolescent Clinic
Dept. of Pediatrics
University of Alabama
Medical Center
Birmingham, AL 35294
(205) 934-4961

ARIZONA
Adolescent Clinic
Arizona Health Services
University of Arizona
1501 North Campbell
   Avenue
Tucson, AZ 85724
(602) 626-0111

CALIFORNIA
Adolescent Clinic
Naval Regional Medical
   Center
Camp Pendleton, CA 92055
(714) 725-5556

CALIFORNIA (Continued)
Leo J. Ryan Teen Clinic
Guadalupe Health Center
75 Willington Street
Daly City, CA 94014
(415) 755-7740

Adolescent Clinic
445 South Cedar Street
Fresno, CA 93702
(209) 453-5201

Adolescent Clinic
Children's Hospital of Los
   Angeles
4650 Sunset Boulevard
Los Angeles, CA 90027
(213) 669-2153

L.A. Co. Dept. of Health
Probation Health Division
Adolescent Clinic, Rm. #104
1601 Eastlake Avenue
Los Angeles, CA 90033
(213) 226-8723

CALIFORNIA *(Continued)*
Adolescent Clinic
Kaiser Foundation Hospital
12500 South Hoxie Avenue
Norwalk, CA 90650
(213) 920-4881

Teen Clinic
Oakland Children's Hospital
51st at Grove Avenue
Oakland, CA 94609
(415) 654-8363

Adolescent Clinic
Kaiser Foundation Hospital
13652 Cantara Street
Panorama City, CA 91402
(213) 781-2361

Adolescent Medical Clinic
UCSD, Medical Center
225 West Dickinson Street
San Diego, CA 92103
(714) 294-6786

Adolescent Clinic
Balboa Naval Hospital
San Diego, CA 92134
(714) 233-2318

Adolescent Clinic
Child and Youth Project
Mt. Zion Hospital
1600 Divisadero Street
San Francisco, CA 94120
(415) 567-6600

Adolescent and Youth Clinics
University of California
Medical Center
400 Parnassus Avenue
San Francisco, CA 94143
(415) 666-2184

CALIFORNIA *(Continued)*
Youth Clinic
San Francisco General
  Hospital
1001 Potrero Avenue
San Francisco, CA 94110
(415) 821-8376

Adolescent Clinic
Children's Hospital
3700 California Street
San Francisco, CA 94119
(415) 387-8700

Adolescent Youth Clinic
Children's Hospital
520 Willow Road
Stanford, CA 94304
(415) 317-4800

Adolescent Clinic
Harbor UCLA Medical
  Center
1000 West Carson Street
Torrance, CA 90509
(213) 533-2317

COLORADO
Adolescent Clinic
University of Colorado
Medical Center
4200 East 9th Avenue
Denver, CO 80220
(303) 394-8461

Westside Teen Connection
990 Federal Blvd., 2nd Floor
Denver, CO 80204
(303) 292-9690

Adolescent Medical Clinic
Fitzsimons Army Medical
  Center

COLORADO *(Continued)*
Aurora, CO 80232
(303) 341-8879

Valley Wide Health Service
P.O. Box 778
Alamosa, CO 81101
(303) 589-3658

CONNECTICUT
Child and Adolescent
   Service
Mount Sinai Hospital
500 Blue Hills Avenue
Hartford, CT 06112
(203) 242-4431

Adolescent Clinic
Yale New Haven Hospital
789 Howard Avenue
New Haven, CT 06510
(203) 436-3616

Adolescent Unit
Bridgeport Hospital
267 Grant Street
Bridgeport, CT 06602
(203) 384-3064

DISTRICT OF COLUMBIA
Adolescent Medicine Clinic
Howard University Hospital
2041 Georgia Avenue, N.W.
Washington, DC 20060
(202) 745-1376

Adolescent Medicine
Children's Hospital, National
111 Michigan Avenue, N.W.
Washington, DC 20010
(202) 745-5464

DISTRICT OF COLUMBIA
(Continued)
Child and Youth Ambulatory
   Services
Georgetown University
   Medical Center
3800 Reservoir Road
Washington, DC 20007
(202) 625-7452

Adolescent Clinic
Walter Reed Army Medical
   Center
Washington, DC 20012
(202) 576-1107

HAWAII
Adolescent Program
Kapiolani Children's Medical
   Center
1319 Punahou Street
Honolulu, HI 96826
(808) 947-8511

Adolescent Unit
Straub Clinic and Hospital
888 South King Street
Honolulu, HI 96813
(808) 523-2311

Adolescent Clinic
Tripler Army Medical Center
Honolulu, HI 96859
(808) 433-6326

IDAHO
Nampa Clinic
1515 Third Street, N
Nampa, ID 83651
(208) 466-7869

IDAHO *(Continued)*
Parma Clinic
311 Grove, Box 45
Parma, ID 83660
(208) 722-5147

Homedale Clinic
116 East Idaho Street
Homedale, ID 83628
(208) 337-3189

ILLINOIS
Adolescent Clinic
Rush Presbyterian Hospital
1753 West Congress Parkway
Chicago, IL 60612
(312) 942-5000

Doc's Corner
500 Racine
Chicago, IL 60607
(312) 829-0046

Adolescent Medical Clinic
Michael Reese Hospital
29th Street at Ellis Avenue
Chicago, IL 60616
(312) 791-2000

IOWA
Adolescent Clinic
Departments of Medicine
   and Pediatrics
University of Iowa Hospitals
Iowa City, IA 52242
(319) 356-2229

KENTUCKY
Adolescent Clinic/GYN
   Clinic
Division of Adolescent
   Medicine

KENTUCKY *(Continued)*
Norton Children's Hospital
Louisville, KY 40202
(502) 589-8750

MARYLAND
Adolescent Clinic
Montgomery County Health
   Department
8500 Colesville Road
Silver Spring, MD 20910
(301) 565-7729

Adolescent Clinic
Wing 5-C
University of Maryland
   Hospital
22 South Greene Street
Baltimore, MD 21201
(301) 528-5400

MASSACHUSETTS
Adolescent and Young Adult
   Medicine
Children's Hospital Medical
   Center
300 Longwood Avenue
Boston, MA 02115
(617) 734-6000

Adolescent Clinic
Tufts New England Medical
   Center
171 Harrison Avenue
Boston, MA 02111
(617) 956-5000

Adolescent Center
Boston City Hospital
818 Harrison Avenue
Boston, MA 02118
(617) 424-6086

90

MASSACHUSETTS *(Continued)*
Adolescent Clinic
Kennedy Memorial Hospital
Brighton, MA 02135
(617) 254-3800

Teen Health Services
St. John's Hospital
Hospital Drive
Lowell, MA 01852
(617) 458-1411

MICHIGAN
Internal/Adolescent
    Medicine
3rd Floor, Out-Patient
    Building
University Hospital
Ann Arbor, MI 48109
(313) 763-5170

Adolescent Ambulatory
    Services
Children's Hospital of
    Michigan
3901 Beaubien Boulevard
Detroit, MI 48201
(313) 494-5762

Adolescent Clinic
Hurley Medical Center
1 Hurley Plaza
Flint, MI 48502
(313) 766-0193

MINNESOTA
Community University
    Health Care Center
2016 16th Avenue, South
Minneapolis, MN 55404
(612) 376-4774

MINNESOTA *(Continued)*
Teenage Medical Services
2425 Chicago Avenue
Minneapolis, MN 55404
(612) 874-6125

Face-to-Face
716 Mendota Street
St. Paul, MN 55106
(612) 772-2557

MISSISSIPPI
Adolescent Medicine
    Services
Keesler AFB Medical Center
Keesler AFB, MS 39534
(601) 377-3766

Rush Clinic
1314 19th Avenue
Meridian, MS 39301
(601) 483-0011

MISSOURI
Adolescent Clinic
Children's Mercy Hospital
240 Gillham Road
Kansas City, MO 64108
(816) 471-0626

NEBRASKA
Adolescent Clinic
Omaha Childrens
12808 Augusta Avenue
Omaha NE 68144
(402) 330-5690

Weight Loss Clinic
Children's Memorial
    Hospital
44th at Dewey Avenue
Omaha, NE 68105
(402) 553-5400

NEW JERSEY
Adolescent Clinic
Monmouth Medical Center
Long Branch, NJ 07740
(201) 222-5200

Adolescent Services and
Clinic
Morristown Memorial
Hospital
100 Madison Avenue
Morristown, NJ 07960
(201) 540-5199

Adolescent Clinic
Martland Hospital
100 Bergen Street
Newark, NJ 07103
(201) 456-5779

NEW YORK
Adolescent Medical Program
Brookdale Hospital Medical
Center
Linden Blvd. at Brookdale
Plaza
Brooklyn, NY 11212
(212) 240-6452

Division of Adolescent
Medicine
Montefiore Hospital and
Medical Center
111 East 210th Street
Bronx, NY 10467
(212) 920-4045

Adolescent and Young Adult
Oncology Unit
Roswell Park Memorial
Institute

NEW YORK (Continued)
666 Elm Street
Buffalo, NY 14263
(716) 845-4560

Adolescent Medicine
Long Island-Jewish Hillside
Medical Center
New Hyde Park, NY 11042
(212) 470-2756

Adolescent Medical Unit
Pediatric Project
550 First Avenue
New York, NY 10016
(212) 561-6321

Child and Youth Project
Roosevelt Hospital
428 West 59th Street
New York, NY 10019
(212) 554-7475

Adolescent Health Center
The Door
618 Avenue of the Americas
New York, NY 10011
(212) 691-6161

Adolescent Health Center
Mt. Sinai Medical Center
19 East 101st Street
New York, NY 10029
(212) 831-1127

Adolescent Clinic
New York Hospital, Cornell
525 East 68th Street
New York, NY 10021
(212) 472-5454

W. F. Ryan Teen Center
160 West 100th Street
New York, NY 10025
(212) 865-7661

NEW YORK *(Continued)*
Adolescent Clinic
601 Elmwood Avenue
Rochester, NY 14642
(716) 275-2962

Threshold
115 Clinton Avenue, South
Rochester, NY 14604
(716) 454-7530

General Adolescent Clinic
Onondaga County Health
    Department
Family Planning
Civic Center
Syracuse, NY 13210

Adolescent Services
Westchester County Medical
    Center
Valhalla, NY 10595
(914) 347-7570

NORTH DAKOTA
Fargo Clinic
737 Broadway
Fargo, ND 58102
(701) 237-2431

OHIO
Adolescent Clinic
Pavilion Building
Children's Hospital, Medical
    Center
Elland & Bethesda Avenues
Cincinnati, OH 45229
(513) 559-4681

Price Hill Clinic
741 State Avenue
Cincinnati, OH 45204
(513) 251-4600

OHIO *(Continued)*
Mt. Auburn Health Center
1947 Auburn Avenue
Cincinnati, OH 45219
(513) 241-4949

Millvale Clinic
3301 Beekman
Cincinnati, OH 45225
(513) 681-3855

Lincoln Heights Health
    Center
1171 Adams Avenue
Cincinnati, OH 45215
(513) 771-7801

Findlay Market Clinic
19 West Elder
Cincinnati, OH 45210
(513) 621-4400

Adolescent Clinic
Cleveland Metropolitan
    General Hospital
3395 Scranton Road
Cleveland, OH 44109
(216) 398-6000

Adolescent Diagnostic
    Center
Cleveland Clinic Foundation
9500 Euclid Street
Cleveland, OH 44118
(214) 444-5616

Teen Health Center
St. Vincent Hospital and
    Medical Center
2213 Cherry Street
Toledo, OH 43608
(419) 259-4795

93

OKLAHOMA
Adolescent Medicine Clinic
Children's Memorial
  Hospital
940 N.E. 13th Street, Room
  1B511
Oklahoma City, OK 73190
(405) 271-6208

PENNSYLVANIA
Adolescent and Youth Center
801 Old York Road, Suite 222
Jenkintown, PA 19046
(215) 887-1678

Adolescent Medical Center
1723 Woodbourne Road, #10
Levittown, PA 19057
(215) 946-8353

Adolescent Clinic
Children's Hospital
34th & Civic Center
  Boulevard
Philadelphia, PA 19104
(215) 387-6311

SOUTH CAROLINA
Medical Park Pediatrics and
  Adolescent Clinic
3321 Medical Park Road
Columbia, SC 29203
(803) 779-7380

Adolescent Clinic
Greenville General Hospital
701 Grove Road
Greenville, SC 29605
(803) 242-8625

TEXAS
Adolescent Clinic
Children's Medical Center
1935 Amelia Street
Dallas, TX 75235
(214) 637-3820

Adolescent Clinic
Robert B. Green Hospital
527 North Leona Street
San Antonio, TX 78207
(512) 223-6361

Adolescent Referral Clinic
University of Texas
Health Services Center
7703 Floyd Curl Drive
San Antonio, TX 78284
(512) 691-6551

Adolescent Clinic
University of Texas
Medical Branch
Galveston, TX 77550
(713) 765-1444

Adolescent Clinic
Ben Taub Hospital
Ben Taub Loop
Houston, TX 77071
(713) 791-7000

Chimney Rock Center
6425 Chimney Rock Road
Houston, TX 77071
(713) 526-5701

Adolescent Medical Services
William Beaumont Army
  Medical Center
El Paso, TX 79920
(915) 569-2121

TEXAS *(Continued)*
Adolescent Medical Services
Brooke Army Medical Center
Ft. Sam Houston, TX 78234
(512) 221-6735

VIRGINIA
Adolescent Medicine
Children's Hospital of the
  Kings Daughters
800 West Olney Road
Norfolk, VA 23507
(804) 622-1381

Adolescent Clinic
Pediatric Services
Naval Regional Medical
  Center
Portsmouth, VA 23708
(804) 397-6541

Adolescent Medical Clinic
Medical College of Virginia
Box 151—MCV Station
Richmond, VA 23298
(804) 786-9408

WASHINGTON
Adolescent Clinic
Group Health Co-op of Puget
  Sound
10200 First Street, N.E.
Seattle, WA 98125
(206) 545-7138

Rainier Youth Clinic
Child and Youth Project
3722 South Hudson Street
Seattle, WA 98118
(206) 587-4650

Adolescent Clinic
University of Washington

WASHINGTON *(Continued)*
Division of Adolescent
  Medicine
Seattle, WA 98105
(206) 545-1274

Adolescent Health Clinic
Tacoma Pierce County
  Health Department
Tacoma, WA 98405
(206) 593-4100

Adolescent Clinic
Madigan Army Medical
  Center
Tacoma, WA 98431
(206) 967-7082

WISCONSIN
Beaumont Clinic
1821 South Webster Avenue
Green Bay, WI 54301
(414) 437-9051

Teenage Clinic
Clinical Sciences Center
600 Highland Avenue
Madison, WI 53792
(608) 263-6406

Marshfield Clinic
Adolescent Section and
  Clinic
1000 North Oak
Marshfield, WI 65549
(715) 387-5413

Child and Adolescent Health
  Center
Milwaukee Children's
  Hospital
1700 West Wisconsin Avenue
Milwaukee, WI 53233
(414) 931-4105

I.O.D.E. Children's Centre
North York General
4001 Leslie Street
Willowdale, Ontario M2K
   1E1
(416) 492-3336

Adolescent Clinic
Hospital for Sick Children
555 University Avenue
Toronto, Ontario M5G 1X8
(416) 597-1500

Child and Adolescent
   Services
3666 McTavish Street
Montreal, Quebec H3A 1YA
(514) 392-5022

CANADA *(Continued)*
Adolescent Unit
Montreal Children's Hospital
2300 Tupper Street
Montreal, Quebec H3H 1P3
(514) 937-8511

Miriam Kennedy Child and
   Family Clinic
509 Pine Avenue, W
Montreal, Quebec H2W 1S4
(514) 849-1315

Adolescent Clinic
Ste-Justin Hospital
3175 Cote Ste-Catherine
Montreal, Quebec H3T 1C5
(514) 731-4931

For Children's Services, call your state or local Mental
Health Association, your pediatrician, or your local hospital.